THE
CIVIL WAR

THE
CIVIL WAR

Books in this series include:

THE CIVIL WAR

BY DON NARDO

LUCENT
BOOKS®

THOMSON
GALE

San Diego • Detroit • New York • San Francisco • Cleveland • New Haven, Conn. • Waterville, Maine • London • Munich

© 2003 by Lucent Books. Lucent Books is an imprint of The Gale Group, Inc., a division of Thomson Learning, Inc.

Lucent Books® and Thomson Learning™ are trademarks used herein under license.

For more information, contact
Lucent Books
27500 Drake Rd.
Farmington Hills, MI 48331-3535
Or you can visit our Internet site at http://www.gale.com

LIBRARY OF CONGRESS CATALOGING-IN-PUBLICATION DATA

Nardo, Don, 1947–
    The Civil War / by Don Nardo.
        p. cm. — (The history of weapons and warfare)
Summary: Discusses the weapons of American Civil War soldiers and different means of warfare used during that conflict.
    Includes bibliographical references and index.
    ISBN 1-59018-068-2 (alk. paper)
  1. United States—History—Civil War, 1861–1865—Technology—Juvenile literature. 2. United States. Army—Weapons systems—History—19th century—Juvenile literature. 3. Confederate States of America. Army—Weapons systems—History—19th century—Juvenile literature. 4. Military weapons—United States—History—19th century—Juvenile literature. [1. United States—History—Civil War, 1861–1865. 2. United States. Army—Weapons systems—History—19th century. 3. Confederate States of America. Army—Weapons systems—History—19th century. 4. Weapons—History—19th century.] I. Title. II. Series.
    E491.N37 2003
    973.7'3—dc21

                                   2002011032

Printed in the United States of America

Contents

Foreword

The earliest battle about which any detailed information has survived took place in 1274 B.C. at Kadesh, in Syria, when the armies of the Egyptian and Hittite empires clashed. For this reason, modern historians devote a good deal of attention to Kadesh. Yet they know that this battle and the war of which it was a part were not the first fought by the Egyptians and their neighbors. Many other earlier conflicts are mentioned in ancient inscriptions found throughout the Near East and other regions, as from the dawn of recorded history city-states fought one another for political or economic dominance.

Moreover, it is likely that warfare long predated city-states and written records. Some scholars go so far as to suggest that the Cro-Magnons, the direct ancestors of modern humans, wiped out another early human group—the Neanderthals—in a prolonged and fateful conflict in the dim past. Even if this did not happen, it is likely that even the earliest humans engaged in conflicts and battles over territory and other factors. "Warfare is almost as old as man himself," writes renowned military historian John Keegan, "and reaches into the most secret places of the human heart, places where self dissolves rational purpose, where pride reigns, where emotion is paramount, where instinct is king."

Even after humans became "civilized," with cities, writing, and organized religion, the necessity of war was widely accepted. Most people saw it as the most natural means of defending territory, maintaining security, or settling disputes. A character in a dialogue by the fourth-century B.C. Greek thinker Plato declares:

> All men are always at war with one another. . . . For what men in general term peace is only a name; in reality, every city is in a natural state of war with every other, not indeed proclaimed by heralds, but everlasting. . . . No possessions or institutions are of any value to him who is defeated in battle; for all the good things of the conquered pass into the hands of the conquerors.

Considering the thousands of conflicts that have raged across the world since Plato's time, it would seem that war is an inevitable part of the human condition.

War not only remains an ever-present reality, it has also had undeniably crucial and far-reaching effects on human society and its development. As Keegan puts it, "History lessons remind us that the states in which we live . . . have come to us through conflict, often of the most bloodthirsty sort." Indeed, the world's first and oldest nation-state,

8

Egypt, was born out of a war between the two kingdoms that originally occupied the area; the modern nations of Europe rose from the wreckage of the sweeping barbarian invasions that destroyed the Roman Empire; and the United States was established by a bloody revolution between British colonists and their mother country.

Victory in these and other wars resulted from varying factors. Sometimes the side that possessed overwhelming numbers or the most persistence won; other times superior generalship and strategy played key roles. In many cases, the side with the most advanced and deadly weapons was victorious. In fact, the invention of increasingly lethal and devastating tools of war has largely driven the evolution of warfare, stimulating the development of new counter-weapons, strategies, and battlefield tactics. Among the major advances in ancient times were the composite bow, the war chariot, and the stone castle. Another was the Greek phalanx, a mass of close-packed spearman marching forward as a unit, devastating all before it. In medieval times, the stirrup made it easier for a rider to stay on his horse, increasing the effectiveness of cavalry charges. And a progression of late medieval and modern weapons—including cannons, handguns, rifles, submarines, airplanes, missiles, and the atomic bomb—made warfare deadlier than ever.

Each such technical advance made war more devastating and therefore more feared. And to some degree, people are drawn to and fascinated by what they fear, which accounts for the high level of interest in studies of warfare and the weapons used to wage it. Military historian John Hackett writes:

An inevitable result of the convergence of two tendencies, fear of war and interest in the past, has seen a thirst for more information about the making of war in earlier times, not only in terms of tools, techniques, and methods used in warfare, but also of the people by whom wars are and have been fought and how men have set about the business of preparing for and fighting them.

These themes—the evolution of warfare and weapons and how it has affected various human societies—lie at the core of the books in Lucent's History of Weapons and Warfare series. Each book examines the warfare of a pivotal people or era in detail, exploring the beliefs about and motivations for war at the time, as well as specifics about weapons, strategies, battle formations, infantry, cavalry, sieges, naval tactics, and the lives and experiences of both military leaders and ordinary soldiers. Where possible, descriptions of actual campaigns and battles are provided to illustrate how these various factors came together and decided the fate of city, a nation, or a people. Frequent quotations by contemporary participants or observers, as well as by noted modern military historians, add depth and authenticity. Each volume features an extensive annotated bibliography to guide those readers interested in further research to the most important and comprehensive works on warfare in the period in question. The series provides students and general readers with a useful means of understanding what is regrettably one of the driving forces of human history—violent human conflict.

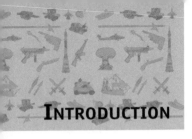
The First Modern War?

Looking back on the American Civil War, one cannot help being struck by the enormous and appalling loss of life that occurred during the conflict. More than 3 million soldiers took part in the Civil War between 1861 and 1865. The armies of the Union and Confederacy engaged in about fifty major battles and perhaps five thousand minor ones. More than 623,000 soldiers died, and at least 100,000 civilians lost their lives. These losses were greater than those sustained by Americans in the American Revolution, War of 1812, Mexican-American War, Spanish-American War, World War I, World War II, and Korean War combined. In a single day—during the Battle of Antietam, in September 1862—There were some twenty-seven thousand casualties, more than on any other day in the country's history. That is four times the number of soldiers who died in the bloody landings on the beaches of Normandy (in France) on D day (June 6, 1944) in World War II.

Sudden Advances in Weaponry

The Civil War's staggering numbers of casualties occurred in part because the conflict was fought at a pivotal time in the history of weapons and warfare. Before the industrial revolution, which profoundly transformed European and American society in the first half of the nineteenth century, technological advances in weaponry, transportation, and communication had been fairly slow and constant over the course of many centuries. Weapons had long consisted of swords, spears, crude and inaccurate guns, and old-fashioned sailing ships. On land, transportation was accomplished by foot or horse. And news and war communications were carried by messengers on horseback.

In response to relatively minor changes in these areas over the years, military commanders had needed to adjust their strategies and battle tactics only slightly from time to time. By contrast, some historians claim, Civil War generals failed to adjust adequately to the sudden and major advances in weaponry (particularly faster-firing, more accurate rifles) that took place in the decades immediately preceding the conflict. Scholar Joe Kirchberger sums up this view:

> Gunpowder and firearms had been introduced into warfare in the 14th century, and very little change had taken place in the use of arms for hundreds of years since. It has been observed that a soldier of the 15th or 16th century could have appeared during the Napoleonic wars [in Europe in the early nineteenth century] and not have found any weapon he could not understand or operate. Weapons changed radically in the

Hundreds of dead soldiers lie in a sunken road near Sharpsburg, Maryland, following the battle of Antietam, one of the bloodiest battles of an incredibly bloody war.

1840s when the fruits of the Industrial Revolution were beginning to be applied to warfare. For instance, the effective range of firearms had been greatly extended. One explanation of the horrifying casualties of the Civil War is that generals, who belonged to an older generation, were using old military tactics of attack, although the ranges of rifles and artillery [cannons] had greatly increased, rendering the attacking forces much more vulnerable than they had been before.[1]

Other experts contend that this scenario is somewhat exaggerated, pointing out that the newer weapons were either in short supply or still mechanically imperfect or unsophisticated. So, there was no need for commanders to institute radical changes in traditional battlefield tactics.

One reason for the appalling loss of life in the conflict was that soldiers in long lines fired at one another in the open at close range, as in the battle of Shiloh, seen here.

Even if this second view is the more accurate one, it cannot be denied that new, more lethal weapons began to change the face of war, and in the process took a frightful toll. The use of such weapons in increasing numbers by both sides in the Civil War contributed to a lengthening of the conflict by keeping one side from gaining an overpowering advantage over the other. Relatively small numbers of defenders were able to hold off or repel considerably larger numbers of attackers, some of whom had similar weapons, especially when the defenders hid behind protective barriers. These factors made many battles indecisive and almost always bloody. Such outcomes are usually associated with modern conflicts, such as World Wars I and II; in these wars, both sides were armed with extremely lethal weapons and used similar tactics, making a swift, clear-cut victory almost impossible to achieve and causing enormous numbers of casualties. It is not surprising, therefore, that many modern historians and other experts have called the Civil War the first modern war. Noted Civil War historian Paddy Griffith writes,

The apparent failure of attacking armies to defeat defending armies, even when there was a heavy numerical advantage in favor of the attack, has often been hailed as the dividing line between the warfare of the past and that of the present, the moment at which Napoleonic conditions ceased to apply and First World War conditions took over. . . . The conditions of Napoleonic warfare seem to have been most favorable to the strategic attacker, those of the First

World War least favorable. The Civil War apparently comes in somewhere half-way between the two, but still with little less than an even chance of victory for the offensive. [2]

Early Fruits of Industry and Technology

Thanks to the industrial revolution, other new and developing technological advances became key factors contributing to the scope and lethality of the fighting, as well as the modernity, of the Civil War. It was the first war in which railroads played a significant role, for example. In 1850, the United States had only about nine thousand miles of tracks laid, but by the outbreak of the Civil War, a mere decade later, that number had risen to almost thirty-one thousand. Generals sometimes transported large numbers of troops long distances swiftly by rail, and trains moved large quantities of badly needed food and other supplies. Several battles were fought to seize control of vital railway connections.

The telegraph was another technological marvel that proved to be a crucial factor in the conflict. The Civil War was the first war in which commanders sent and received important messages via advanced communications. A fair proportion of the Union victory can be attributed to the fifteen thousand miles of telegraph lines established in the Northern states.

Other advances in technology that made the Civil War different than previous wars could be seen in the fighting at sea and on rivers. For the first time, steamships, metal-armored warships, and submarine torpedoes became major factors in warfare. "It was an unorthodox and often wild naval war," remarks naval historian A.A. Hoehling.

The Civil War was waged at sea with more massed violence and with more diversity of ships and weaponry than any previous, sustained naval action. . . . Iron or tin plating was nailed onto wooden steamships to make them "ironclads" or "tinclads." Still they took their knocks from . . . shore batteries [land cannons] and from ingenious mines (or "torpedoes"). . . . The war at sea was demanding, real, and frightening, even though casualties were dwarfed by those in the great land battles.[3]

Considering all of these factors, an examination of the weapons of the Civil War reveals numerous technological changes

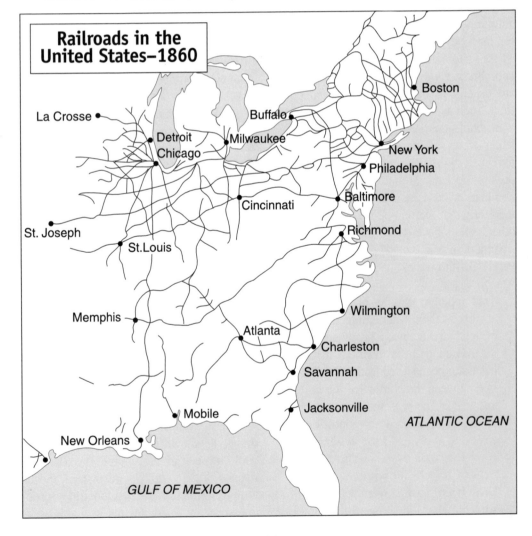

Railroads in the United States–1860

and new inventions that came together in one place at one time. Such innovations made it easier for soldiers to kill one another faster than had been possible in the past. And the conflict's grim casualty figures show that huge numbers of soldiers did die.

However, this does not mean that all of the carnage is attributable simply to the lethality of weapons and other advances in technology. As late as 1864, a year before the war's end, many kinds of weapons were in short supply and a hodgepodge of modern and outdated weapons still existed on most battlefields. Not surprisingly, the soldiers carrying outdated weapons were more likely to be killed if their opponents had better arms. Perhaps just as important was the very nature of the war. Countrymen were pitted against countrymen, and brother against brother, each side convinced that its cause was both just and paramount. Self-righteousness, stubbornness, and savagery were inevitable in such a fight.

Of course, shortages of weapons and civil hatreds have not been limited to modern wars. Thus, the Civil War's claim to being the first modern war, if in fact it was, rests mainly on the fact that it utilized, in varying degrees, the early fruits of industry and technology.

CHAPTER ONE

Muskets and Rifles

The vast majority of handheld weapons used in the Civil War were firearms. Swords and bayonets saw little use in combat, mainly because opposing troops usually fired at each other from a distance of a few hundred feet or more and rarely got close enough for hand-to-hand combat. Of 7,302 men wounded during one of Union general Ulysses S. Grant's major campaigns, only six were injured by swords or bayonets. A lowered bayonet could and often did intimidate and frighten an enemy, but it rarely actually killed him. Telling are these lines from the diary of Oscar Jackson, a Union officer, describing an incident in the 1862 Battle of Corinth: "Corporal Selby, then a private, killed a rebel with his bayonet . . . which is a remarkable thing in a battle and was spoken of in the official report."[4]

Of the main firearms used in the war—muskets and rifles, or "long arms"—there was a wide, even bewildering variety. Some loaded from the muzzle (the front of the barrel), others from the breech (the back of the barrel). They featured a number of different firing mechanisms and calibers. (The caliber of a gun is the specific width of its bore, or inside of its barrel.) Also, some were designed for use by infantry (foot soldiers), others for cavalry (soldiers on horseback).

One of the disturbing realities of the war was that many of these weapons were manufactured in prior eras and were obsolete, or nearly so, when the conflict began; in fact, out-of-date weapons remained widespread during the first two or three years of fighting. This use of outdated weaponry hampered efforts to standardize weapons systems and caused many unnecessary deaths. Eventually, large numbers of Union soldiers and a smaller proportion of Confederates obtained better weapons, some of which were produced by government-sponsored factories, others bought from Europe, and still others captured from the enemy.

Weapons from the Past

The oldest long arms carried by the combatants in the first few years of the war were "smoothbore" muskets. The term musket originally referred to a gun with a long barrel whose bore had a smooth surface (from which, the word smoothbore derived). A large number of smoothbore muskets saw service in the Civil War. Two of the more prevalent examples were the Model 1816/1822 and Model 1840 muskets. (The years indicated are those in which the guns were manufactured and/or issued by the U.S. Army.) The 1816/1822 musket had a barrel about fifty-seven inches long, a caliber of .69 inches, and weighed about nine pounds; the 1840 model had almost identical specifications. Both were muzzle loaders, meaning that soldiers loaded them by inserting the musket balls (round lead bullets) into the front of the barrel. Large num-

bers of both of these guns eventually ended up in the armories of state militias. So when the Civil War started, the Union and Confederacy, both desperate for weapons to arm their soldiers, issued as many of them as they could find.

Part of the reason such muskets were outdated is that they used an old-fashioned firing mechanism called the flintlock, which was not always reliable and required several steps to load. The flintlock first appeared in the mid- to late 1600s. It worked by causing a piece of flint to hit a steel plate, which would produce a spark that in turn ignited some gunpowder in a small pan mounted in the breech of the weapon. According to military historian Archer Jones,

In this old-fashioned flintlock mechanism, the spring-loaded hammer (right center) is primed to strike the steel plate (left center), which is itself attached to the powder pan.

HARD TO FIND GOOD WEAPONS

The Comte de Paris, a French officer who served on the staff of Union general George McClellan, wrote a detailed history of the war. Here, he tells why the North had some difficulties in acquiring good weapons, especially in its dealings with European arms merchants.

The young historian, the Comte de Paris, poses proudly in his Union uniform.

The wonderful machines by which the most complicated rifles now in use throughout Europe are constructed almost without the aid of man are of American invention, and have given a well-deserved reputation to the expansion rifles manufactured at the government armory in Springfield. But this establishment had only capacity for producing from ten to twelve thousand yearly, and the supply could not be increased except by constructing new machines. The private workshops were equally insufficient; the Federal factory at Harper's Ferry had been destroyed by fire, and the depots were empty. It was important, however, to supply the most pressing of all the wants of the soldier, that of having a weapon in his hands. During the first year of the war the ordnance department succeeded in furnishing the various armies in the field, not counting what was left at the depots, one million two hundred and seventy-six thousand six hundred and eighty-six portable firearms (muskets, carbines, and pistols), one thousand nine hundred and twenty-six field- or siege-guns, twelve hundred pieces for batteries in position, and two hundred and fourteen million cartridges for small-arms and for cannon. But it was obliged to apply to Europe for muskets and ammunition; this was the only war commodity that America procured in considerable quantities from the Old World, and it was this supply which proved to be the most defective. Agents without either experience or credit, and sometimes unscrupulous, bought in every part of Europe, on account of the Federal government, all the muskets they could pick up, without any regard to their quality or price.

The flint, held by the spring-loaded hammer, struck a blow against a plate attached to the cover of the pan, opening the pan as it simultaneously caused sparks which ignited the powder and fired the musket. . . . The flintlock greatly increased the rate of fire [as compared to earlier, even slower firing mechanisms], a process speeded up by the use of an oblong paper cartridge that contained the ball and the proper amount of powder. . . . With a flintlock the musketeer bit off the end of the cartridge with his teeth, retaining the ball in his mouth; used some powder from the cartridge to fill the pan and poured the remainder down the barrel, following it with the ball from his mouth and the paper of the cartridge; he then used his ramrod [a wooden or metal stick] to drive the paper and ball down on the powder, and he was ready to fire. Instead of one round a minute, the soldier with a flintlock with paper cartridge could fire two or three or even more rounds in a minute.[5]

Although a soldier could fire two or three times per minute with a flintlock musket, he could expect at least one out of every five shots to misfire or not fire at all. Also, the gun's accuracy was poor beyond a range of about a hundred yards. This meant that it was not very useful as a long-range weapon.

A more reliable firing mechanism, based on the percussion cap, appeared between 1807 and 1814. It consisted of a metal hammer attached to the gun and a metal (usually copper) plate, or "cap," that the operator placed over a small tube, or "nipple," in the barrel's breech. The cap was coated with a chemical, potassium chlorate. When the operator pulled the trigger, the hammer struck the cap, which flashed, igniting the gunpowder and firing the weapon.

The percussion system was more reliable than the flintlock because the caps only rarely failed to spark and fire the gun. Percussion guns were also simpler and cheaper to make than flintlocks. However, for a long time, military leaders worried that soldiers would have too much trouble applying the small cap to the nipple. So they did not order large numbers of percussion guns until 1842, when a .69-caliber percussion musket was manufactured. After that, the army slowly began to refit, or convert, some of its older flintlocks to the percussion system. The armory in Springfield, Massachusetts, for example, refitted almost twenty-seven thousand 1840 flintlocks between 1849 and 1851; most of these saw service in the Civil War.

Some older muskets were refitted with a more advanced percussion system—the Maynard primer, which used caps coated with an explosive chemical called fulminate. "The tape primer worked rather like a child's roll-cap pistol," military historian Ian Drury explains.

A paper tape containing fulminate patches was fed over the nipple by the action of the hammer. . . . Fitting a [standard] percussion cap was a fiddly business, especially with cold hands, or when under stress. Maynard's primers were cranked into place automatically. . . . Unfortunately, [Maynard's system] was not

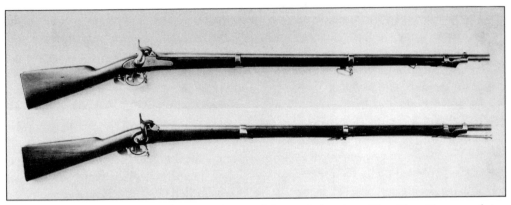

The upper gun, a .69-caliber Palmetto musket, and the one below it, a .70-caliber Morse musket, were both made before the Civil War.

wholly reliable, since if the paper tape became damp, it failed to feed properly.[6]

Advantages and Disadvantages of Rifles

Whether fired by a flintlock or percussion cap, the musket's most serious disadvantage was that it was not very accurate. The weapon's bore was smooth. And for various reasons, the musket ball was smaller than the bore. For example, several smoothbore muskets issued by the U.S. Army in the early nineteenth century, including the 1816/1822 and 1840 models, had a bore .69 inches in diameter but fired a ball .64 inches across. The space between the edge of the ball and inside of the barrel, in this case .05 inches, is called windage; even a small amount of windage can create big problems. As explained by William B. Edwards, an expert on nineteenth-century firearms,

Bullets that were undersized had the habit of bounding down the barrel on discharge, striking first one point on the bore and then another. When the bullet left the muzzle it might strike yards off the target, in any direction, depending on the last bounce it made in its hectic journey from breech to muzzle. This was wholly unpredictable and resulted in poor accuracy.[7]

This drawback of smoothbore firearms was largely eliminated in another kind of gun—the rifle, which was used more extensively in the Civil War than any other type of gun. The term *rifle* is derived from the weapon's "rifling," a set of spiral grooves etched into the inside walls of the barrel. When the weapon was fired, the ball spun through the grooves and exited the gun spinning; at the same time, the ball fit tightly in the bore, almost eliminating the windage. The result was a much more accurate shot.

Another advantage of the rifle was its greater range and velocity, also a result of the ball's tighter fit. The windage of the ball in a musket allowed some of the gas produced by the exploding gunpowder to rush

20

past; thus, some of the propulsive power of the gas was wasted. In the rifle, by contrast, the ball was lodged firmly in the rifling. This sealed all the gas behind it and took advantage of nearly all of the explosive power of the gunpowder.

Despite these advantages, the rifle had been far less common than the less-accurate musket, especially on the battlefield. Although rifles began to be used by some American hunters and frontiersmen in the early 1700s, these weapons saw only limited use in the American Revolution, mainly in the hands of specially trained snipers, and no major attempt to mass-produce rifles for military use was made before the 1850s. This was because the rifle had two serious disadvantages. First, it took much longer to load a rifle than it did a smoothbore musket. The rifleman first had to first force the ball into the rifling near the gun's muzzle, often with a mallet, and then use his ramrod to push it farther down into the barrel. The result was that most riflemen could get off only one shot per minute, or two at best. The second problem

Though muskets were inaccurate and rifles slow to load, both weapons could be lethal, as evidenced by the grisly remains of soldiers at Cold Harbor, Virginia.

was that a small residue of gunpowder coated the barrel's grooves each time the weapon fired; after several shots, the residue began to "foul" the barrel, which then had to be cleaned.

Weapon designers worked long and hard to find a way to speed up the rifle's loading process. One obvious solution was to make a bullet that was small enough for the operator to insert easily into the barrel. However, such a bullet would be *too* small to conform to the rifling after the weapon was fired. What was needed was a small bullet that expanded in size at the right moment. The breakthrough came in the late 1840s when a French military officer, Captain Claude-Etienne Minié, introduced what came to be called the Minié bullet in his honor. According to Ian Drury,

> The bullet had a hollow base with an iron plug inserted. Although it did not engage the rifling on its way down the barrel, the moment the rifle was fired, the bullet expanded. The hard iron plug was driven violently into the softer lead, forcing it against the sides of the barrel as it raced toward the muzzle.[8]

The Advent of the Rifle Musket

The combination of rifling and the Minié bullet rendered the old smoothbore muskets obsolete. And the U.S. military soon decided that all new firearms it ordered would be rifled. Because these new weapons combined the best features of muskets and rifles, they came to be called "rifle muskets." In 1855, the army ordered production of a muzzle-loading .58-caliber rifle musket that used a percussion firing system. The intent was for these guns to become the military's standard infantry weapon. Plans were laid to phase out the older smoothbores and flintlocks by refitting them with rifling and percussion or by selling them to gun collectors.

This slow process had barely begun when the Civil War broke out in April 1861. At that time, modern rifle muskets accounted for only about 10 percent of the total long arms in American arsenals. By midsummer 1861, Union quartermasters had issued all of the 1855 .58 caliber versions, along with most of the .69-caliber converted and unconverted smoothbores. As the war widened, both the Union and Confederacy became desperate for guns, especially up-to-date ones.

The upper weapon is a Richmond rifle musket, dating from 1863. Below it is a Cook rifle musket, made in Athens, Georgia, in 1864.

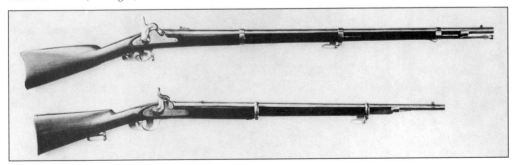

In July 1861, soon after the start of the war, Union workers in a munitions factory make cartridges for muskets. Millions of cartridges were made during the conflict.

One solution was to step up production of new rifle muskets. In 1861, the Springfield armory began production of the Model 1861, a .58-caliber percussion gun that became the most common handheld firearm used in the war. Thereafter, these guns bore the generic name "Springfields," even though many were manufactured at other armories. The Union made or bought well over 1 million Springfields between 1861 and 1865.

Meanwhile, the South tried to keep pace. However, it lacked the industrial capacity of the North. (On the eve of the war, 110,000 of the country's 128,000 factories were in the North, and nearly all of the gunpowder and cannons were produced in the North.) The Confederate armories at Fayetteville, North Carolina, and Richmond, Virginia, began turning out small numbers of their own version of the 1861 .58 rifle musket,

along with other assorted muskets and rifles. In his memoirs, Edward P. Alexander, a high-ranking Confederate artillery officer, remembered the South's chronic problem of limited supplies of up-to-date guns. In the war's early stages, he recalled,

> We had great trouble with the endless variety of arms and calibers in use, scarcely ten percent of them being the muzzle-loading rifle musket, caliber .58, which was then the regulation arm for the United States infantry. . . . The old smoothbore musket, caliber .69, made up the bulk of the Confederate armament at the beginning, some of the guns, even all through 1862, being old flintlocks. But every effort was made to replace them by rifled muskets captured in

Typical Civil War Long Arms

Weapon	Effective Range (in yards)	Theoretical Rates of Fire (in rounds/minute)
U.S. rifled musket, muzzle-loaded, .58-caliber	400–600	3
English Enfield rifled musket, muzzle-loaded, .577-caliber	400–600	3
Smoothbore musket, muzzle-loaded, .69-caliber	100–200	3

battle. . . . Not until after the battle of Gettysburg [in 1863] was the whole [Confederate] army in Virginia armed with the rifled musket.[9]

Another way that both the Union and Confederacy attempted to make up for such shortages was by purchasing guns from Europe. The North bought more than 1.1 million European rifles and muskets, including 436,000 of what became the second most widely used infantry firearm of the conflict—the British Enfield .577-caliber rifle musket. Except for the small difference in caliber, it closely resembled the American-made 1861 .58 model and became very popular among Northern soldiers. Southern soldiers liked Enfields, too, and the Confederacy bought more than 300,000 of them during the course of the war.

Breechloaders and Carbines

In his recollections of the difficulties of weapons procurement, Edward Alexander also stated, "In 1864 we [the Confederates] captured some Spencer breech-loaders, but we could never use them for lack of proper cartridges."[10] This reference to breechloaders is telling. No matter how advanced their rifling and firing mechanisms, muzzle-loading guns had some serious drawbacks. In particular, it was not uncommon under stressful combat conditions for soldiers to make mistakes during the complex loading process. Some rammed their bullets down the barrel before inserting the powder; others accidentally inserted multiple bullets; and still others left their ramrods in the barrel.

By contrast, loading a gun through the breech required no ramrod. And because only one bullet could be loaded at a time, there was no danger of overloading the weapon. Breechloaders had been around for a long time. But because of difficulties in manufacture and other problems, they had not seen wide military use. Then, in 1848, a young American mechanic named Christian Sharps introduced a new and improved breech-loading rifle with a caliber of .52 inches that was relatively simple to make and use. It was also faster to load than any muzzle loader; a foot soldier armed with a Sharps rifle could get off as many as six to nine shots per minute.

When the Civil War broke out, however, the Union did not adopt breechloaders in large quantities for its infantry. This was mainly because the officer in charge of supplying firearms, James W. Ripley, was a conservative, old-fashioned individual who believed that the guns he had grown up with were superior to most "newfangled" models. He is reported to have remarked,

Below, a .52-caliber Sharps carbine (top) and a .54-caliber Burnside carbine; right, a close-up of the Burnside's mechanism.

A great evil now especially prevalent in regard to arms for the military service is the vast variety of new inventions, some in my opinion unfit for use as military weapons and none as good as the United States musket.[11]

Thanks to Ripley, the Sharps infantry rifle saw only limited use in the war. The federal government ordered fewer than ten thousand of them.

However, even Ripley could not deny that breechloaders were more practical than

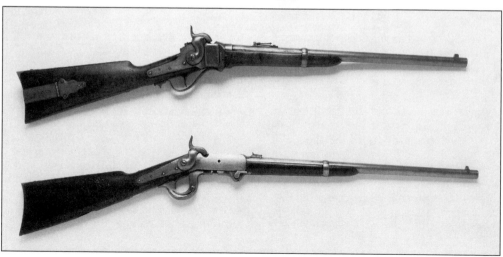

muzzle loaders for the cavalry. After all, dealing with a gun, cartridges, percussion caps, and a ramrod, all while holding the reins of a horse, was impractical—if not impossible—for a man riding into battle. So, during the course of the war, the Union ordered more than eighty thousand Sharps .52-caliber carbines for the cavalry. (Designed specifically to lighten a cavalryman's burden, a carbine was a somewhat shorter and lighter version of a standard infantry rifle.) Ripley also ordered some fifty-five thousand .54-caliber Burnside breechloading carbines and smaller quantities of other carbines.

The Revolutionary Spencer Repeater

One thing all these carbines had in common was that they were single-shot breechloaders; that is, the horseman loaded a cartridge, fired, and then repeated the process at will. More devastating and revolutionary was the repeating rifle, or "repeater," a breechloader that used cartridges containing more than one bullet and loaded the bullets into the firing chamber automatically. The Spencer repeater (named after its inventor, Christopher M. Spencer), which came in several calibers, including .52 inches, proved to be the most widely used and most coveted breechloader of the Civil War. The Comte de Paris, a French officer who fought on the Union side in the conflict, later described the weapon this way:

> The Spencer rifle [is] an excellent arm, the use of which became more and more extended in the Federal [Union] army. The butt [back end] is pierced, in the direction of the length, by a tube containing seven cartridges, which are deposited successively, after each fire, in the chamber, replacing in turn those which, when discharged are thrown

NOT ENOUGH BREECHLOADERS

In this tract from his memoirs, Edward P. Alexander, a high-ranking Confederate artillery officer, describes the shortage of breechloaders and repeating rifles during the conflict.

There were several [faster-firing] breechloading small arms manufactured at the North, but none had secured the approval of the United States Ordnance Department, although many of them would have made more formidable weapons than any muzzle-loaders. The old idea was still widely entertained that, because the percentage of hits [in a battle] was always small, the fire of infantry should not be rapid, lest the men waste too much ammunition. After a year or two, some of the best breech-loaders got admission among cavalry regiments, and common sense and experience gradually forced a recognition of the value of a heavy fire. By 1864, the Spencer breech-loading carbine had been adopted as the regulation arm for the Federal cavalry, and by the fall of that year brigades of infantry began to appear with it. . . . There is reason to believe that had the Federal infantry been armed from the first with even the breechloaders available in 1861, the war would have been terminated within a year.

This is a close-up view of a carbine equipped with a Maynard primer. The exposed round socket held a rolled tape of patches coated with fulminate, an explosive chemical.

out by a very simple mechanism. This magazine [ammunition holder], entirely protected, is very easily recharged. Many extraordinary instances have been cited of successful personal defense due to the rapidity with which this arm can be fired, and some Federal regiments of infantry which made a trial of it were highly pleased with the result. Most of these rifles were of two models—one for the use of the infantry, the other [a carbine], lighter and shorter, for the cavalry. [12]

The federal government purchased a total of eighty-five thousand Spencer carbines. And several thousand more were bought by states and individual soldiers who desperately wanted to replace their older guns with this superior weapon. It could fire up to twenty or so rounds per minute, making the soldier who carried it a fighting machine of unprecedented power and lethality. As with other breechloaders, however, the conservative and stubborn Ripley did not see the potential of the new gun for use by the infantry. And he did everything he could to block production of

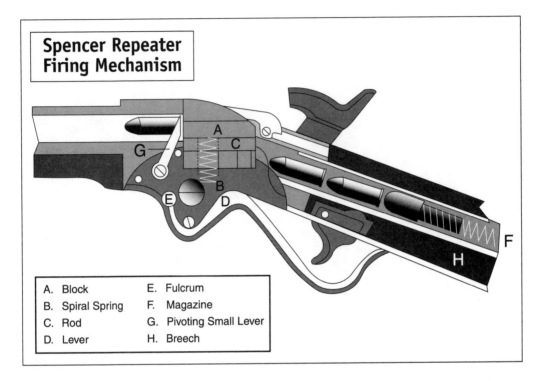

Spencer Repeater Firing Mechanism

A. Block
B. Spiral Spring
C. Rod
D. Lever
E. Fulcrum
F. Magazine
G. Pivoting Small Lever
H. Breech

Spencer infantry rifles. Ripley retired in September 1863 and, fortunately for the Union, his successors, George D. Ramsey and Alexander B. Dyer, did recognize the potential of breechloaders for infantry. But the war ended before large numbers could be made and issued. As it was, one man's lack of vision had changed the course of history. If repeating rifles had been issued to Northern soldiers as their standard weapon starting in 1861, the Union may well have defeated the Confederacy in a year, or two at most.

CHAPTER TWO

Artillery Guns
and Batteries

Though handheld firearms were the most common weapons used in the Civil War, both sides regularly utilized bigger guns, generally referred to as cannons but more formally called artillery or heavy ordnance. There were many individual types of artillery. Overall, however, they were divided into two general classes: field artillery, which were light and mobile enough to move from place to place along with the infantry and cavalry; and heavy or siege artillery, much heavier guns that usually remained in fixed positions and fired on towns and ships at sea.

Both the Union and Confederacy used such big guns in more or less the same ways. What distinguished the artillery corps of the two sides was a tremendous difference in size and tactical effectiveness. Because most of the industrial capacity of the United States was concentrated in the North at the start of the war, the Union possessed a clear advantage in production of heavy ordnance. The North had more raw materials, including iron and other metals for gun barrels and cannonballs and minerals for making gunpowder; more factories for making cannons and ammunition; and far more trained mechanics.

General Henry Hunt, chief of the Union artillery, later summed up the situation this way:

> While the South had at the beginning of the war the better raw material for infantry and cavalry, the North had the best for artillery. A[n artillery] battery requires many mechanics with their tools and stores, and also what are called handy men. No country furnishes better men for the artillery proper than our Northern, and particularly our New England, states. [13]

At the beginning of the conflict, the North had 163 cannons and rapidly manufactured thousands more.

In contrast, when the war started, the South possessed fewer than fifty operational

Union workers forge metal pieces for cannon carriages in an arsenal in West Troy, New York.

cannons. And many of these had been made during the War of 1812, so they were terribly outdated. In addition, even though the Confederacy managed to build facilities for making artillery, it could not keep pace with or match the Union's output of cannons and ammunition. Edward Alexander, the Confederate officer who complained about the South's shortage of modern rifle muskets, also pointed out its frequent lack of effective artillery:

> Our artillery equipment at the beginning was even more inadequate than our small-arms. Our guns were principally smoothbore 6-pounder and 12-pounder howitzers, and their ammunition was afflicted with very unreliable fuses. Our arsenals soon began to manufacture rifled [artillery]

guns, but they always lacked the copper and brass [bronze], and the mechanical skill necessary to turn out first-class ammunition. Gradually we captured Federal guns to supply most of our needs, but we were handicapped by our own [lack of] ammunition until the close of the war. [14]

At first, the South also lacked experienced artillery officers and gunners. Most had to learn on the job, which resulted in many mistakes, missed opportunities, and unnecessary deaths.

Artillery Guns

Whether already experienced or learning on the job, both Union and Confederate artillery gunners dealt with the same physical and mechanical realities of their specialized weaponry. Those who handled field artillery learned that there were two major types: "guns" and howitzers. Both were cast from iron or bronze (sometimes colloquially but inaccurately referred to as "brass"). Also, both could be either smoothbore or rifled, like handheld muskets and rifles, and both types of field cannons were usually muzzle-loading. (Breech-loading artillery pieces were rarely used in the Civil War because their mechanisms, still in a primitive state of development, were awkward and often unreliable.)

What differentiated artillery guns from howitzers was their design and application. The gun had a long barrel in relation to its caliber and was usually used for firing at targets within plain sight, as on an open battlefield. Also, the weapon's trajectory—the path taken by its projectile—was flat, or not too high. The gunner aimed the weapon by sighting along two notches, one located near the muzzle, the other near the breech. He also had to use his experience to estimate the range of the target and the angle to which the gun's barrel had to be tilted to

A rare photo of the Tredegar Iron Works, in Richmond, Virginia. For a long time it was the only Confederate facility capable of casting cannon barrels.

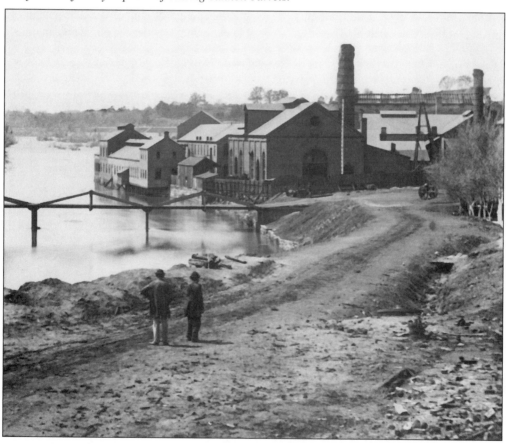

achieve that range, since no mechanical range-finding aids yet existed. If he wanted less elevation (to make the cannon shoot lower, with a flatter trajectory), he twisted a screw mechanism, the "elevating screw," mounted on the underside of the barrel's breech.

The artillery gun's flat trajectory and line-of-sight flight path made it a fairly effective weapon when used in the open against an oncoming line of enemy troops. According to Ian Drury,

> On gently sloping, hard ground, gunners learned to bounce their shot according to the range so that it could plow into closely packed infantry formations at chest height. The faster

the shot traveled, the further [sic] it could reach. Even rolling along the ground, a cannonball could be deceptively dangerous; their momentum could smash the unwary ankle or break a carriage wheel.[15]

Still, relatively few soldiers were actually hit by iron cannonballs (technically known as solid shot), which made them the least lethal type of ammunition fired by artillery guns. The three other major types of ammunition were shells, spherical case, and canister, all of which could, if aimed well, inflict more casualties per shot than cannonballs. Shells were essentially hollowed-out cannonballs containing charges of gunpowder. The danger of the exploding powder to people and animals,

A Civil War howitzer stands on display at Fort Pulaski, Georgia. Howitzers had shorter barrels and fired at a higher angle than artillery guns.

DANGER OF BEING CRUSHED

In his memoirs, published in 1975 as Gone for a Solider, *Union private Alfred Bellard commented on the confusion and danger caused by the large numbers of swiftly moving artillery batteries in and around the bloody battle at Malvern Hill, fought on July 1, 1862.*

At the foot of the hill, at Malvern Hills Tavern, the artillery, baggage wagons and infantry were in a disorganized mass, all jumbled together without regularity or purpose and everyone [was] for himself. The artillery was driven along the road as fast as the horses could pull it, and the infantry had to keep their eyes open, and get out of the way to avoid being run over or crushed to death between two guns. The mud in some places was over our boots.

except at very close range, was minimal; much more damage was done by flying pieces of the iron container or by secondary explosions caused when the shells ignited ammunition stores. Spherical case and canister shot also consisted of hollow containers. As suggested by its name, a container for spherical case was round; also known as shrapnel or grape shot, it held many small lead or iron musket balls that scattered in all directions after a fuse ignited a charge of gunpowder packed inside. A round of spherical case for a twelve-pound gun contained seventy-eight balls; a round for a six-pounder contained thirty-eight balls. (The poundage of an artillery piece most often referred to the weight of the shot it fired; thus, a twelve-pound gun usually fired a missile weighing twelve pounds.) Canister shot also contained metal balls and/or whatever metal scrap could be found; the difference was that the container was cylindrical, like a can.

Artillery Howitzers and Napoleons

Whereas guns fired all four kinds of shot, howitzers, the second major type of field ar-

tillery, fired only shells, case, and canister. A howitzer could fire at a higher angle than a gun. This was partly because the howitzer had a larger caliber and shorter barrel, which made it easier to maneuver on a carriage. The weapon had a bigger caliber and shorter barrel because it was designed to fire shells. Being hollow, a shell was more fragile than solid shot, so the charge that propelled the shell had to be smaller to keep it from rupturing the shell's casing. The smaller the explosion, the shorter the barrel length needed to accommodate it. The barrel of an average howitzer was five to seven times its caliber, compared to fifteen to twenty-five times for a gun.

Because they were designed to fire at higher angles than guns, howitzers were the cannons of choice when one needed to fire over obstacles like trees, houses, and low hills to reach the target. However, to hit the target was difficult. To begin with, often one could not actually see it. Also, determining the proper range was tricky. If an artillery crew miscalculated the range of a round of solid shot, it did not matter much; the cannonball would still keep going and at

The Union and Confederacy both manufactured Napoleon cannons like this one.

least disrupt part of an oncoming enemy line. But if the range of a howitzer shell fell short of the enemy, the explosion did no damage and was wasted.

Before the advent of the Civil War, the U.S. Army made up for the individual shortcomings of guns and howitzers by mixing a few of each together in a typical artillery battery. Shortly before the outbreak of the war, however, the army developed a field artillery piece that featured some of the more important advantages of both a twelve-pound gun and a howitzer. In 1857, experimental trials were held with five "Napoleons," named after the famous French emperor who had used artillery to great effect in Europe earlier in the same century. The Napoleon was a twelve-pound smoothbore artillery gun with a caliber of 4.62 inches. It was shorter and

lighter than a traditional twelve-pounder, making it more like a howitzer than a gun. It could also fire shells at a slightly higher angle than a gun, although not as high as an average howitzer.

The Napoleon performed so well that it became the most widely used cannon of the Civil War. The Union ordered 179 Napoleons in 1861 after the beginning of the war; by the end of the conflict, it had produced 1,131 of them. The Confederacy manufactured a total of 630 of their own version of the weapon (distinguished from the Union model by a lack of flare, or widening, at the muzzle). In 1862, Confederate general Robert E. Lee recommended that old-style six-pound guns and twelve-pound howitzers be melted down to make new twelve-pound Napoleons.

Advantages and Drawbacks of Rifled Cannons

Both the North and South also used rifled cannons. Like handheld rifles, artillery pieces with rifled bores had longer ranges and were more accurate than smoothbores. Consequently, two rifled cannons saw wide use, mainly (though not exclusively) by the Union. These were ten- and twenty-pound Parrott guns (named after their inventor, Robert Parrott) and three-pounders. The Parrott guns had many admirers, who praised their unprecedented range and accuracy. "There is perhaps no better system of rifled cannon," wrote Northern general Quincy Gilmore. "Certainly none [is] more simple in construction, more easily understood, or that can, with more safety, be placed in the hands of inexperienced men for use."[16]

Many of the gunners who actually operated the Parrotts disagreed with this assessment, however. They reported that the barrels tended to burst more often than they should, causing unwarranted injuries and deaths. In fact, in a battle fought at Fort Fisher, North Carolina, in December 1864, more Union soldiers were killed by their exploding Parrott guns than by enemy fire.

Rifled cannons had other drawbacks as well. Their long range was a benefit mainly in flat, unencumbered landscapes; not surprisingly, they were not very useful in wooded, hilly terrain. Also, because of their unusual range and power, they often drove shells deep into the ground, where they exploded harmlessly. After taking part in an artillery duel in the first Battle of Bull Run in July 1861, Confederate general J.D. Imboden wrote,

An artillery train of rifled Parrott guns maneuvers onto a battlefield. These weapons were known for their accuracy, but some gunners considered them unsafe.

The shot and shell of the rifles [i.e., rifled cannons], striking the ground at any angle over fifteen or twenty degrees, almost without exception bored their way in several feet and did no harm. It is no exaggeration to say that hundreds of shells from these fine rifleguns exploded in front of and around my battery that day, but so deep in the ground that the fragments never came out. After the action the ground looked as though a drove of hogs had been rooting there for potatoes. I venture the opinion here, after a good deal of observation during four years, that in open ground at 1000 yards a six-pounder battery of smooth [bore] guns, or at 1500 to 1800 yards, a similar battery of 12-pounder Napoleons, well handled, will in one hour whip double their number of the best rifles ever put in the field. A smoothbore gun never buries its projectiles in the ground, as the rifles do invariably when fired against sloping ground.[17]

Artillery Batteries and Crews

Whether the cannons were smoothbore or rifled, or fired solid shot, shells, or canisters, the main tactical unit of all field artillery used in the Civil War was the battery. (With some variations, four batteries made up an artillery division and several divisions made up an artillery corps.) A typical battery had six field pieces, either guns or howitzers or a mix of the two, though four-piece batteries were not uncommon.

The officer in charge of a battery was usually a captain; under him were two or three lieutenants, each commanding two pieces, which made up a section of the battery. Each piece was operated by a lead gunner and seven assistant gunners (or artillerymen). All

This contemporary photo shows a Union artillery battery under the command of a captain named Winslow, at Fredericksburg, Virginia, May 2, 1863.

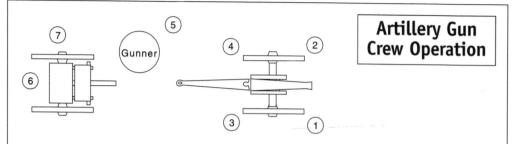

Artillery Gun Crew Operation

During firing, the eight-man artillery crew took their positions as shown in the diagram above. At the command "commence firing" the gunner ordered "load" and sighted the gun. # 1 sponged the bore, #5 received a round from #7 at the limber and carried it to #2 who placed it in the bore. # 1 rammed the round to the breech while #3 placed a thumb over the vent to prevent premature detonation of the charge. After gun was loaded #3 inserted a vent pick in the vent that punctured the cartridge bag. # 4 attached a lanyard to a friction primer and inserted the primer in the vent. At the command "fire" #4 yanked the lanyard to the fire. # 6 cut fuses for exploding shells when needed.

The Four Basic Types of Ammunition

SHOT: Cast iron with no explosive charge. Used against cavalry, troops in column formation, buildings and other solid objects. Long range.

SHELL: Round, hollow projectile with a powder-filled cavity. Fused; exploded into 5–12 larger pieces. Long range.

SPHERICAL CASE: Hollow shell filled with powder and 40–80 musket balls that exploded in all directions. Fused; used at a range of 500–1500 yards.

CANISTER: A tin can containing 27–78 iron balls packed in sawdust. Can ripped open at the muzzle when fired. Range of 50–300 yards. Turned cannon into a giant shotgun.

of these men not only fought as a coordinated unit but also traveled, ate, and slept together. Noted Civil War scholar Jack Coggins describes such a field artillery battery on the march:

Each gun or "piece" was hooked up behind a limber [a two-wheeled cart for pulling cannons], which carried an ammunition chest, and was drawn by six horses. Each piece had its caisson [a two-wheeled cart for carrying ammunition], carrying three ammunition chests, and also drawn by a six-horse team. These two units made a platoon, commanded by a sergeant (chief of piece) and two corporals. Each battery was accompanied by a traveling forge, a battery wagon carrying tents and supplies, and usually six more caissons carrying reserve ammunition. . . . Each six-horse team had three drivers, who rode the horses on the left side. The usual gun crew consisted of nine men. If the battery was designated as light artillery, the cannoneers either rode on the ammunition chests or walked beside their piece. If it was horse artillery (sometimes called flying artillery) the cannoneers each rode a horse. Two additional men acted as horse-holders in action.[18]

The members of a battery maintained this same sort of cohesiveness and cooperation in combat. For the sake of maximum efficiency, the members of a gun crew were numbered and followed a strict series of steps when loading their weapon. When the lead gunner gave the order to load, artilleryman Number 1 used a sponge at the end of a wooden pole to swab out any gunpowder residue lingering inside the barrel; meanwhile, Numbers 6 and 7, who stood beside the limber, handed the cannonball, shell, or canister to Number 5, who carried it to the piece. There, Number 2 took the ammunition from him and inserted it into the barrel's muzzle; Number 1 rammed the shot down the barrel; then Number 3 aimed the cannon according to the lead gunner's directions, while Number 4 primed a small vent in the side of the breech with powder. On the lead gunner's order to "Fire!" Number 4 ignited the charge, firing the weapon. All were careful to stand clear because when the piece discharged, it jumped violently backward, since efficient recoil mechanisms had yet to be invented. The crew then pushed the piece back into position as quickly as they could and repeated the loading process.

Sustaining and Inflicting Damage

Injuries from the recoil or an occasional exploding barrel were not the only potential dangers for an artillery crew. In the heat of battle, enemy infantry and cavalry tried to knock out as many artillery batteries as they could. Whenever possible, units of one's own infantry and cavalry did their best to protect the artillery batteries. But sometimes a battery was caught in the open with enemy soldiers advancing on it. At the Battle of Spotsylvania, in May 1864, Battery C, 5th U.S. Artillery, found itself in such a situation and was torn to pieces by enemy fire, as later described by one of its two surviving members:

Lieutenant Metcalf gave the command . . . and away we went, up the hill, past our infantry, and into position [in the open in sight of the enemy]. . . . We were a considerable distance in front of our infantry, and of course artillery could not live long under such a fire as the enemy were putting through there. Our men went down in short order. The left gun fired nine rounds, I fired fourteen with mine. . . . Our section went into action with 23 men and one officer. The only ones who came out sound were the lieutenant and myself. Every horse was killed, 7 of the men were killed outright, 16 wounded; the gun carriages were so cut with bullets as to be of no further service. . . . 27 balls passed through the lid of the limber chest while Number six was getting out ammunition. The sponge bucket on my gun had 39 holes in it, being perforated like a sieve. [19]

Despite such bloody incidents, it was more often the case that artillery batteries, especially those of the Union, inflicted far more damage than they sustained. Perhaps

the most dramatic example occurred on July 1, 1862, at Malvern Hill, near the James River in Virginia. The huge Union artillery division, consisting of at least 250 pieces, was stationed on the hill. After these batteries mauled the less numerous Confederate guns, wave after wave of Southern infantry charged up the hill, only to be mowed down by the Northern artillery. More than five thousand Confederate soldiers lost their lives in a hideous bloodbath. One of the Confederate generals who took part, D.H. Hill, later remembered the loss of one of his gun batteries:

> The woods around us [were] filled with shrieking and exploding shells. I noticed a [Southern] artillery man

Part of the massive Union artillery division that fought at Malvern Hill in July 1862. These cannons mowed down wave after wave of attacking Confederate troops.

seated comfortably behind a very large tree, and apparently feeling very secure. A moment later a shell passed through the huge tree and took off the man's head.[20]

Later that day, as the Southern infantry brigades marched to their doom, one "retreated in disorder," Hill said. Another was "streaming to the rear," while still another was "suffering heavily and effecting little." Hill recalled grimly, "It was not war—it was murder."[21]

Mortars Create Chaos

Another type of artillery was the mortar, one of the principal siege cannons used in the war. (Large-caliber Parrotts and other big guns were also employed to attack towns and forts.) A mortar was a short, stumpy cannon that fired at high angles, allowing its shells to pass over the high walls of forts and fortified towns and drop downward on the desired target. Most mortars had barrels only one to three times their calibers in length, so if a mortar's caliber was ten inches, its barrel was

Flanked by the members of its battery, the Union mortar known as the "Dictator" stands before Petersburg in October 1864.

ENDURING THE SHELLING OF VICKSBURG

Incredibly, sometimes the people inside a besieged town managed to go on with their lives even while subjected to deadly barrages of artillery shells. Here (from Joe Kirchberger's The Civil War and Reconstruction), *Edward S. Gregory, a resident of Vicksburg, Mississippi, remembers the shelling of that city in June 1863.*

Just across the Mississippi . . . mortars were put into position and trained directly on the homes of the people. . . .

Twenty-four hours of each day these preachers of the Union made their touching remarks to the town. . . . The women and children of Vicksburg took calmly and bravely the iron storm. . . . They became at last such an ordinary occurrence of daily life that I have seen ladies walk quietly along the streets while the shells burst above them, their heads protected meanwhile by a parasol held between them and the sun.

---

somewhere between ten and thirty inches long.

The most widely used mortar of the Civil War was the Coehorn (named after its Dutch inventor). The Coehorn had a caliber of 5.82 inches and a barrel only a little more than 16 inches long. Though regularly called a twenty-four-pounder, it fired shells weighing seventeen pounds, which could reach as far as twelve hundred yards. Other mortars used in the conflict had eight- and ten-inch calibers and ranges of up to 4,250 yards. The largest of all mortars that saw service in the war was a Union weapon nicknamed the "Dictator." It had a caliber of thirteen inches and fired shells weighing 220 pounds as far as 4,350 yards.

The spectacle, confusion, and fear that mortars and other big siege cannons could create was well illustrated in the war's opening salvo—the Confederate attack on Union-controlled Fort Sumter (in Charleston Harbor, South Carolina, in April 1861). According to a reporter for the *Charleston Observer,* "Shell followed shell in quick succession; the harbor seemed to be surrounded by miniature volcanoes belching forth fire and smoke."[22] Union soldier Abner Doubleday, who was in the fort, later wrote that, on April 12:

Our firing now became regular and was answered from the rebel guns which encircled us on four sides. . . . When the immense mortar shells, after sailing high in the air, came down in a vertical direction and buried themselves in the parade ground, their explosion shook the fort like an earthquake.[23]

The next day, said Doubleday:

The scene at this time was really terrific. The roaring and crackling of the flames, the dense masses of whirling smoke, the bursting of the enemy's shells and our own which were exploding in the burning rooms, the crashing of the shot, and the sound of

Typical Civil War Field Artillery

Weapon	Tube Composition	Tube Length (in inches)	Effective Range at 5° Elevation (in yards)
6-pdr smoothbore field gun 3.67-in. dia. bore	bronze	60	1,523
12-pdr smoothbore field howitzer 4.62-in. dia. bore	bronze	59	1680
12-pdr smoothbore mountain howitzer 4.62-in. dia. bore	bronze	33	1005
10-pdr Parrott rifle 2.9-in. dia. bore	iron	78	1950
3-inch ordnance rifle 3.0-in. dia. bore	iron	73	1835
12-pdr James rifle 3.67-in. dia. bore	bronze	69	1700

masonry falling in every direction, made the fort a pandemonium [place of chaos].[24]

Doubleday's emphasis on the creation of chaos by siege cannons is telling. When the Fort Sumter defenders finally surrendered, none had been killed in the massive barrage, yet they had been badly shaken, which turned out to be the chief effect of such weapons. As Coggins puts it, "While prolonged mortar bombardments did remarkably little actual damage, the moral effect of the screeching shells and noisy bursts was very great, and often drove enemy gunners from their guns."[25]

CHAPTER THREE

Infantry Units and Tactics

F oot soldiers made up the backbone of the armies that clashed in the American Civil War. Cavalry and artillery certainly played important roles, but most often their job was to support and make easier the crucial tasks of the infantry (as well as to damage and harass the enemy infantry). With few exceptions, victory or strategic gain rested on the ability of one's infantry to penetrate, capture, and hold enemy territory.

To understand how the foot soldiers fought, one must first consider how they were organized into units. The basic infantry unit was the regiment. On paper—that is, under ideal conditions—it numbered about a thousand men; however, in the field, most regiments contained considerably fewer men. Battle losses, sickness, absenteeism (men on leave, both official and unofficial), desertion, and the difficulty of finding new recruits all took a toll. In fact, it was not unusual for a regiment to number five hundred or fewer men for varying lengths of time. A typical regiment was divided, again on paper, into ten

companies of one hundred men each, though in the field an average infantry company had only about forty to fifty members. Each company was commanded by a captain and assisted by a first lieutenant and second lieutenant. Individual companies were usually identified by letters, so a soldier might belong to "B Company" or "D Company."

On a higher level, three to six regiments made up a brigade. In the Union army, a brigade was usually commanded by a colonel; Confederate brigades, on the other hand, were led by brigadier generals. Two or three brigades made up a division, commanded in the Union by a brigadier general and in the Confederacy by a major general. And about three divisions made up a corps, commanded by a major general in the North and a lieutenant general in the South. Finally, several corps made up an army. Most often in the Civil War, armies bore the names of localities; for example, the Union had the Army of the Potomac and the Army of the Ohio, while the Confederacy had the

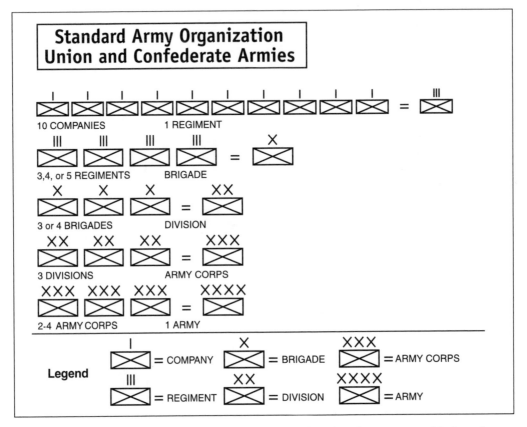

**Standard Army Organization
Union and Confederate Armies**

10 COMPANIES — 1 REGIMENT

3, 4, or 5 REGIMENTS — BRIGADE

3 or 4 BRIGADES — DIVISION

3 DIVISIONS — ARMY CORPS

2-4 ARMY CORPS — 1 ARMY

Legend

= COMPANY   = BRIGADE   = ARMY CORPS

= REGIMENT   = DIVISION   = ARMY

Army of Northern Virginia and the Army of Tennessee.

In combat situations, organization and coordination, especially on the regimental and company levels, were crucial. Commanders recognized the importance of maintaining cohesion among men who trained, traveled, slept, and ate together. The reality was that such comrades in arms would cover one another's backs and take risks for one another more readily than they would for strangers from other units. "Unless a regiment could retain its cohesion in action," Ian Drury points out,

it was doomed to defeat at the hands of a better organized enemy. A dis-

ordered regiment was unlikely to be able to coordinate its fire or maneuver quickly and effectively. Unless order could be reestablished, the regiment would take cover and stay there, unwilling to deliver an attack yet unwilling to give up its ground without a fight. The result would be a long casualty list with little to show for it. [26]

In contrast, when the members of a regiment or company worked together in a coordinated effort, they could execute, to the best of their ability under the existing conditions, the battlefield tactics directed by their commanding officers.

44

Successive Waves of Men

Those tactics varied according to factors such as the lay of the land, the sizes of the opposing forces, the amounts and quality of their weapons and ammunition, and the specific goal of the operation. Most situations, though, witnessed the use of one or two of a few basic kinds of strategy and tactics. When attacking in the open, for example, regiments and brigades usually approached the enemy in successive waves. Most often, each wave was made up of a double line of men separated from the waves in front and behind it by about two hundred yards (although this distance could vary widely). The theory behind this approach was that, if the front wave came under heavy fire, the one behind it was far enough back to remain safe from the bullets, yet the rear wave was also close enough to step forward and take the front one's place if necessary. Unfortunately, under combat conditions, the front waves tended to slow down as they encountered enemy fire. This often caused the succeeding waves to bunch up, creating a large mass of men that was an easy target for enemy riflemen and artillery batteries.

Often, some of the soldiers in the first wave of attackers acted as skirmishers. In a typical regiment, the members of two of the ten companies would move ahead and fan out, usually in widely spaced single file, so that they could patrol the entire battlefield. Their job, a dangerous one, was to probe and test the enemy positions if those positions were hidden or unclear.

The common battle tactic of launching successive waves of men at the enemy appears in this engraving of the Confederate charge up Cemetery Hill at Gettysburg.

Once the skirmishers drew the enemy's fire or otherwise identified the enemy positions, the main body of the first attack wave moved forward. Usually, these men waited until they were closer than a hundred yards to fire the first volley. This and the second volley were extremely important; if these volleys were massive and precise enough, they might cripple or intimidate the enemy enough to send him packing. By contrast, as the number of volleys increased, so did the men's exhaustion and the chances of fouled rifle barrels and other mechanical problems.

The firing distance of a hundred yards or less was not a random decision. Smoothbore muskets, the workhorses of prior wars, had an effective range of fifty to a hundred yards. So if they were fired from farther than a hundred yards, the first and second volleys would be ineffective and wasted. The more modern and accurate rifle muskets did increase the range of lethal fire, but their effect was not major or decisive. Rifles could be extremely accurate at three hundred yards or more. However, this was under ideal conditions, such as in target shooting or when a sniper had the advantage of cover and the time to take careful aim and clean his weapon when the powder built up. In actual combat, powder rapidly fouled rifle barrels, the weapons sometimes misfired, soldiers quickly grew physically fatigued, and many, dazed by the frightening din of battle, made mistakes in loading.

Another drawback of rifles that influenced tactics was their peculiar trajectory. As Drury explains,

A photo shows Union soldiers in battle formation. A line of skirmishers has been deployed in front of the main body of infantry.

MISTAKES MADE IN BATTLE

Standard infantry tactics of any sort were easy to describe in military manuals but often difficult to accomplish in real life, mainly because so many things could go wrong with guns during battle, as explained here by historian Ian Drury (from his Civil War Military Machine*).*

Weapons fired with the ball not fully seated in the breech were liable to misfire or bulge their barrels. The recoil increases in direct proportion to the fouling. After 40 rounds it becomes a major effort to raise the brass-backed rifle stock to a bruised and battered shoulder. In the intense stress of combat, these physical limitations of the weapon were compounded by human error. Some 37,000 muskets were salvaged from the Gettysburg battlefield. Of these, 24,000 were loaded, three-fourths of them with more than one round. The 6000 with just the one round loaded included many weapons with the whole cartridge rammed down unopened, or with the bullet behind the powder charge instead of in front. Some of the multiple-loaded muskets had over half a dozen cartridges hammered down their barrels. Their owners had presumably been going through the motions, but the deafening noise and mind-numbing pressure had dulled their senses. If it is assumed that for every incorrectly loaded rifle left on the field, there was another still slung over someone's shoulder, over a third of the infantry at Gettysburg finished the battle with a disabled weapon.

A bullet aimed at an enemy formation 300 yards away by a kneeling rifleman would pass over 6½ feet above the ground at 200 yards. Dropping low enough to hit a standing man at 250 yards, it would strike the ground 100 yards further [sic] on. This relatively high trajectory meant it was vitally important to estimate the range correctly. [27]

The problem was that estimating range at such distances was extremely difficult, and even the best marksmen sometimes made mistakes. The reality was that rifles increased the effective range of firearms in battle to only about 150 yards at most. "Only hand-picked and expertly trained shots could have hoped to score hits on the Civil War battlefield at much more than 150 yards," Paddy Griffith writes. "But such soldiers were as hard to find as the ammunition needed to give them target practice." [28]

Most commanders did not adjust their tactics to accommodate the slight advantage of rifles over older long arms. They still routinely ordered lines of soldiers to advance on enemy positions and to hold their fire in preparation for one or two massive and crucial volleys at ranges of less than a hundred yards. The result, at least when the enemy was armed with many rifles, particularly breechloaders, was increased numbers of casualties. Yet this adherence to traditional tactics did not prove to be a major impediment to either army in the war. The fact is that many soldiers were not equipped with rifles, especially in the first two or three

Civil War reenactors in the role of Confederates open fire on the Union enemy.

years of fighting, and relatively few infantry soldiers ever carried breechloaders. Also, ammunition shortages, lack of skill in marksmanship, and the stresses of combat all contributed to keeping rifles from realizing their potential. According to Griffith,

> There was no great superabundance of ammunition, least of all in the South. . . . The individual soldier was usually limited to a rather meager supply of cartridges, allowing heavy firing to be sustained by a regiment for only a relatively brief period. An

almost total lack of target practice meant that many rifles were misloaded in combat and that the finer points of long-range accuracy were neglected or ignored. The close-order drill of the day also meant that the soldier in battle was subjected to a barrage of sights, sounds, and emotions which must [have] distracted him powerfully from his task. Even with these wonderful new weapons, in fact, it remains doubtful that a genuine revolution in firepower actually occurred.[29]

MANY PLACES TO HIDE

Trenches were not needed nearly as often as they were dug. As noted historian Paddy Griffith explains from his acclaimed book on Civil War battle tactics, this was mainly because the terrain in the eastern United States provided many hiding places from which infantrymen could fire at the enemy.

Even the most "open" Civil War battlefields actually contained a great deal of cover for the infantryman who went to ground. Just as [the British general] Wellington had concealed his army at Waterloo in an apparently clear field [during the Napoleonic wars], so the American armies habitually covered themselves quite adequately behind such features as a light rail fence, an almost indistinguishable dip in the ground, or even the flimsy protection of standing corn. Each of these could provide a starting-point for a defensive line occupied by soldiers lying prone. If there was a sunken lane, a stone wall, or some similarly solid bulwark, then that would be better still. For an army which could afford to remain static and was not too proud to lie down, almost any piece of ground could quickly be converted into a stronghold, even at close range from the enemy. One did not need a mountain, a forest, or a river line in order to gain security.

A Union sharpshooter uses a tree for cover in this reenactment. Other common forms of cover included boulders, stone walls, wooden fences and sheds, and ditches.

Caught in a Killing Field

The exchange of long-arm fire by infantry at close range was called a firefight. Most often, the two sides simply faced off and blazed away at each other, sometimes for hours, or at least until their ammunition was gone or they were too exhausted to continue. They might then retreat in opposite directions. Or if one side was attacking an entrenched position, the attackers would retreat, leaving the defenders behind their barricades. Sometimes the side with more men left standing was the winner, although more often such engagements ended as stalemates. Sometimes this happened because the men involved showed an unusual degree of discipline and courage. A Union attacker at Champion's Hill, near Vicksburg, Mississippi, in May 1863, later remembered,

The enemy had fallen back a few [yards], forming a solid line parallel to our own, and now commenced in good earnest the fighting of the day. For half an hour we poured the hot lead into each other's faces. We had forty rounds each in our cartridge boxes, and probably nine-tenths of them were fired in that half hour.[30]

Stalemates were not limited to such firefights. The spectacle of armies facing each other at close quarters and periodically fighting with indecisive results became a hallmark of the Civil War. In large part, this is attributable to the most common kind of battlefield tactics that were employed during the conflict—building, defending, and attacking fieldworks. Fieldworks were essentially

Union troops attack Confederates during the battle of Champion's Hill, near Vicksburg, on May 16, 1863.

DISGUSTED WITH HIS GENERAL

Union officer Colonel Emory Upton wrote the following words (quoted in a collection of Upton's letters edited by Peter Michie) to his sister on June 4, 1864, after fighting in the Battle of Cold Harbor.

I am disgusted with the generalship displayed [by General Ulysses S. Grant]. Our men have, in many instances, been ordered upon the enemy's entrenchments, when they knew nothing about the strength or position of the enemy. Thousands of lives might have been spared by the exercise of a little skill; but, as it is, the courage of the poor men is expected to obviate [prevent] all difficulties. I must confess that, so long as I see such incompetency, there is no grade [rank] in the army to which I do not aspire.

fortified trenches, so this approach to fighting is commonly called "trench warfare." The average fieldwork consisted of a ditch dug four to six feet deep with the excavated soil piled up in front as a protective barrier. When enough time and materials were available, the trenches were reinforced with logs and wooden planks and could become quite elaborate. Increasing numbers of trenches were built by both sides as the war dragged on.

Despite their structure and appearance, the main strategy of building these trenches was not simply to provide protection for defensive forces. Rather, fieldworks were designed to force attackers to approach the defenders through an open field of fire in front of the trenches; thus, for a certain amount of time, the attackers would become sitting ducks in a veritable killing field. Indeed, soldiers on both sides learned from experience that heavy casualties were bound to result from assaults on fieldworks. By the last year of the war, many men, especially combat veterans, were reluctant to attack trenches. Some went so far as to refuse direct orders from their superiors to

move against such positions. Consequently, fewer and fewer commanders gave such orders. When they did, and their men obeyed, not surprisingly the results were horrific. This was the case in a series of Union charges against Confederate trenches at Cold Harbor, near Richmond, Virginia, in early June 1864. A Confederate officer, Colonel William Oates, later penned this riveting eyewitness account:

The enemy was within thirty steps. They halted and began to dodge, lie down, and recoil. The fire was terrific from my regiment. . . . The blaze of fire . . . went right into the ranks of our assailants and made frightful gaps through the dense mass of men. They endured it but for one or two minutes, when they retreated, leaving the ground covered with their dead and dying. . . . After the lapse of about forty minutes another charge was made. . . . The charging column . . . received the most destructive fire I ever saw. They were subjected to a front and flank fire from the infantry, at short range, while my piece of artillery poured double charges of canister into them. . . . In two minutes not a man of them was standing. All who were not shot down had lain down for protection. . . . The stench from the dead between our lines and theirs was sickening. It was so nauseating that it was almost unendurable; but we had the advantage, as the wind carried it away from us to them. The dead covered more than five acres of ground about as thickly as they could be laid.[31]

An "Exercise in Exhaustion"

In an effort to avoid such murderous all-out assaults on well-fortified positions, the attackers often "went to ground" by building their own fieldworks. Moreover, it was not unusual for one or even both sides to wait a while and then build new trenches still closer to the enemy. In this way, much of the conflict was subtly transformed from the standard "attack against defense" mode into a contest between fieldwork engineers.

This "exercise in exhaustion,"[32] as one historian calls it, had two important effects on the general tenure of the fighting. First, it needlessly prolonged the war and made much of the conflict indecisive, mainly because both sides were so convinced that digging in provided the best security and, by extension, the best strategy for victory. "If both sides in a war believe that it is impossible to storm [field]works," says Griffith,

then neither side will feel safe until it is sitting behind them, and no one

will wish to put a serious effort into storming the enemy's. Hence both sides will actually have gained security, regardless of any material weaknesses in the trenches themselves, because their beliefs will have turned into a self-fulfilling prophecy. The more strongly those beliefs are held, furthermore, the greater will be the mutual reinforcement and hence the greater military security for the two armies. . . . We can certainly say that on many occasions trenches were dug when they need not have been. . . . They were often used as an excuse to avoid combat by battle-weary soldiers who had been driven too far. . . . They may have saved some lives in the short term, but they also helped to defer [delay] military decisions—and thereby made the war longer and costlier than it might otherwise have been.[33]

Second, the habit of entrenching and/or finding natural hiding places from which to fire at the enemy often made it difficult for attackers to see and concentrate their fire on defenders. A Union infantry captain, John W. de Forest, later recalled the frustration of not knowing the enemy's exact location, especially when that enemy was entrenched:

We were just entering a large open field, dotted by a few trees and thornbushes, with a swampy forest on the right and the levee of the bayou on the left, when the Rebels gave us their musketry [i.e., fired at us]. It was not a volley but a file fire; it was a continuous rattle like that which a boy makes in running a stick along a picket fence, only vastly louder; and meantime the sharp *whit whit* of bullets chippered close to our ears. In the field before us puffs of dust jumped up here and there; on the other side of it a long roll of blue smoke curled upward; to the right of that the gray smoke of artillery rose in a thin cloud; but no other sign of an enemy was visible. [34]

Other Infantry Tactics

Although fieldworks and firefights were the most common tactics used by infantry in the Civil War, other tactics were sometimes employed. One of these was so-called shock action. The idea was to get in close to the enemy and either kill him or force him to flee. In this method, one side dispensed with the

usual static firefight and made a direct assault on the enemy's lines or entrenchments. Bayonets were often used in this situation, but they rarely ended up actually killing anyone. Instead, the sight of a formation of soldiers rushing onward with bayonets lowered was usually enough to intimidate and

At right, part of the formidable fieldworks built to defend Atlanta, Georgia; below, makeshift fortifications near Centerville, Virginia.

frighten the defenders into running. It was the very fact that this tactic was so unorthodox and infrequently used that made it sometimes effective. According to Griffith,

> There is certainly evidence to show that a unit which continued to charge without stopping could cause astonishment in the enemy ranks, simply because such a tactic was so unexpected. Civil War soldiers regarded it as more natural to fight statically by fire, and did not know quite what to make of an attacker who held to some other theory [of combat tactics].[35]

One reason that shock tactics were not used very often during the Civil War was that this approach took unusual courage on the part of both troops and commanders. Direct attacks on enemy lines also required an unusual amount of coordination. If only a handful of the attackers did not keep up with the others and do their jobs well, the whole unit could easily fall apart and the assault fail. Lack of training was another key factor. Most soldiers in the Civil War did little or no drilling in shock action tactics, making this approach less likely to succeed than a standard firefight.

A less audacious variation of shock action was the "Indian rush." A broken line of attackers ran toward the enemy positions, usually bobbing and weaving to make it more difficult for their opponents to shoot them. From time to time, the attackers would fall face down on the ground or hide behind rocks or trees; in these temporary positions they would take a breather and shoot off a few rounds at the enemy; then they would resume their forward rush. Generally speaking, these are common skirmishing tactics. The difference between normal skirmishing and the Indian rush was that the for-

---

THE FUTILITY OF ATTACKING AN ENTRENCHED ENEMY

In a letter to his sister, penned on June 5, 1864 (from Michie's edition of Upton's letters), Emory Upton complains about the futility of attacking a well-entrenched enemy.

We are now at Cold Harbor, where we have been since June 1st. On that day we had a murderous engagement. I say *murderous,* because we were recklessly ordered to assault the enemy's entrenchments, knowing neither their strength nor position. Our loss was very heavy, and to no purpose. Our men are brave, but cannot accomplish impossibilities. My brigade lost about three hundred men. My horse was killed, but I escaped unharmed.

Since June 1st we have been behind rifle-pits, about three hundred yards from the enemy. A constant fusillade [weapons fire] from both sides has been kept up, and, though but little damage has been done, it is, nevertheless, very annoying. I am very sorry to say I have seen but little generalship during the campaign. Some of our corps commanders are not fit to be corporals. Lazy and indolent, they will not even ride along their lines; yet, without hesitancy, they will order us to attack the enemy, no matter what their position or numbers. Twenty thousand of our killed and wounded should today be in our ranks.

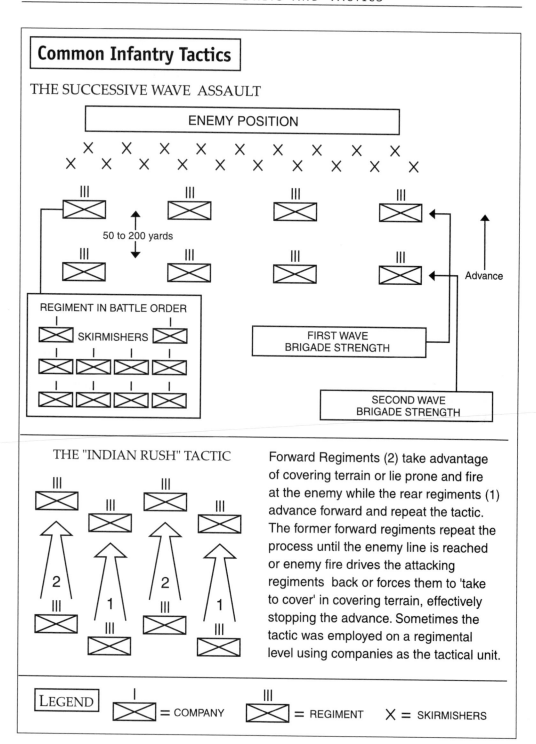

Common Infantry Tactics

THE SUCCESSIVE WAVE ASSAULT

ENEMY POSITION

50 to 200 yards

REGIMENT IN BATTLE ORDER

SKIRMISHERS

FIRST WAVE
BRIGADE STRENGTH

Advance

SECOND WAVE
BRIGADE STRENGTH

THE "INDIAN RUSH" TACTIC

Forward Regiments (2) take advantage of covering terrain or lie prone and fire at the enemy while the rear regiments (1) advance forward and repeat the tactic. The former forward regiments repeat the process until the enemy line is reached or enemy fire drives the attacking regiments back or forces them to 'take to cover' in covering terrain, effectively stopping the advance. Sometimes the tactic was employed on a regimental level using companies as the tactical unit.

LEGEND   = COMPANY   = REGIMENT   X = SKIRMISHERS

mer usually did not end with an assault on the enemy positions, while the latter did.

Frontal assaults were not the only way to overcome enemy positions. More often, soldiers on both sides conducted trench raids. These were usually stealth operations that occurred at night or under the cover of fog and relied on the advantage of surprise. A few dozen, or occasionally a few hundred, men would slip into a trench and capture as many enemy soldiers as possible. The goal was to weaken the defenses, making a subsequent attack by the main body of infantry more likely to succeed.

Still another common tactic used by Civil War foot soldiers was shouting. Battle cries had been used throughout history both to steel the nerves of the attackers and to frighten the enemy. Both sides in the Civil War used them, and sometimes one side tried to outshout the other. One veteran of the conflict later wrote,

At the same time you are ordered to yell with all the power of your lungs. It is possible that this idea may be of great advantage in forcing some of the heroic blood of the body into the lower extremities. Whatever may be the reason, it was certainly a very effective means of drowning the disagreeable yell of the enemy. [36]

One might say that the soldiers yelled because they could. In general, troops in the Civil War, as in any war, used those tactics that were possible and potentially effective within existing limitations. Their guns were only so accurate; their ammunition was in short supply; their training in marksmanship and shock action was minimal; and most of their commanders were learning on the job. It is no wonder that the average foot soldier simply did the best he could with what he had to work with and hoped he would make it home in one piece.

CHAPTER FOUR

Cavalry Units and Tactics

Cavalry played a much smaller role in the Civil War than infantry. But one should not conclude from this fact that horse soldiers were inherently less formidable than or inferior to foot soldiers. Rather, the use of cavalry always depended on the personal views and preferences of individual military commanders. Many, especially in the North, began the war with little appreciation for the potential of cavalry. And in general, neither side provided the money and other resources necessary for creating huge, powerful cavalry units like those that had fought in the Napoleonic Wars in Europe a few decades before. It was not until the last two years of the Civil War that horsemen began to fulfill at least some of their potential as a military weapon.

As the importance of cavalry slowly grew over the war years, a curious reversal of strengths occurred. When the conflict began, the Confederacy had a decided advantage in cavalry. The South was an agrarian society in which men, both young and old, rich and poor, regularly rode, hunted,

and raced on horseback and felt at home in the saddle. Consequently, Confederate commanders had no trouble raising many fine horse soldiers, who supplied their own mounts. Noted Union general William T. Sherman recognized this enemy advantage, commenting,

> The young bloods of the South . . . are brave, fine riders, bold to rashness and dangerous subjects in every sense. . . .
> As long as they have good horses, plenty of forage, and an open country, they are happy. . . . They are the most dangerous set of men that this war has turned loose upon the world. They are splendid riders, first-rate shots, and utterly reckless. [J.E.B.] Stuart, John Morgan, [Nathan B.] Forrest, and [T.J. "Stonewall"] Jackson are the types and leaders of this class.[37]

In contrast, the North was mainly an industrial society in which most horses were used to pull wagons, carriages, or plows.

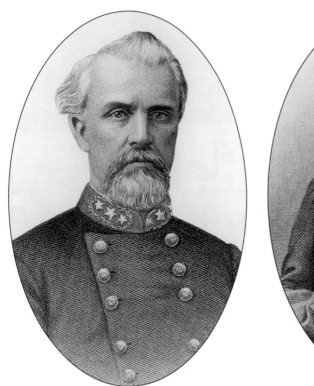

Two of the best and most feared Confederate cavalry commanders of the Civil War—at left Nathan Bedford Forrest, and at right J.E.B. Stuart.

Few Northern men owned horses, had any serious riding experience, or knew the first thing about caring for a horse. Needless to say, the small cavalry units fielded by the Union in 1861 were far inferior to their Confederate counterparts in both confidence and skill.

Yet this situation changed over time. Union horsemen and cavalry commanders learned from their mistakes. They became better organized, and the weapons factories of the industrial North supplied them with more and better weapons than their Southern opponents. Meanwhile, the once strong Southern cavalry declined rapidly. It fell further and further behind the North in pro-

curement of effective firearms. And many horses died in battle or of disease. Because the Confederacy did not subsidize the horses, as the Union did, and replacements were expensive and difficult to find, when a cavalryman's mount died, he often had no choice but to quit the cavalry. One of General Stuart's assistants later wrote,

> We now felt the bad effect of our system of requiring men to furnish their own horses. The most dashing trooper was the one whose horse was the most apt to get shot, and when this man was unable to remount himself he had to go to the infantry service and was lost

to the cavalry. Such a penalty for gallantry was terribly demoralizing.[38]

For these and other reasons, by late 1864 the Union cavalry was not only superior to the Confederate one but the best in the world. Said another Stuart aide, "During the last two years [of the war] no branch of the [Union's] Army of the Potomac contributed so much to the overthrow of Lee's army as the cavalry."[39]

Troops, Regiments, and Corps

A significant part of the initial weakness and later the strength of the Union cavalry lay in the way it was organized into units. In 1861, just prior to the outbreak of the war, five regiments of U.S. cavalry existed. Each regiment was composed of five squadrons of two troops each. Each troop—which was the basic cavalry unit and therefore roughly equivalent to an infantry company—at first had about a hundred men, commanded by a captain and three lieutenants. Shortly after the war started, a new regiment was created, and

each of the six regiments was reorganized into six squadrons of two troops each.

The weakness of this organization was its lack of unity and cohesion. Instead of one giant unit, or corps (like an army infantry corps), that might be used as a single striking force, the cavalry was essentially a group of small individual units, and commanders tended to detach one or two units from the others and assign them separate tasks. Moreover, these tasks were often mundane, such as guarding supply wagons. This was hardly a cost-effective use of soldiers whose mounts and weapons were extremely expensive to buy and maintain.

The situation began to improve significantly, however, after General Joseph Hooker reorganized the Union military in 1862–1863. He eliminated the cavalry squadron and allowed each troop to have as few as eighty-two men, giving these units more flexibility. Each regiment was led by a colonel, assisted by a lieutenant colonel, three majors, three lieutenants, and a regimental surgeon. Four to six regiments now made up a brigade; two to three brigades

---

 # A CAVALRYMAN'S COSTLY NEEDS

A cavalryman's requirements in the field were considerably greater than an infantryman's. Scholar Paddy Griffith explains (from his Battle Tactics of the Civil War).

Cavalry was enormously expensive to feed, and still more expensive to provide with its essential equipment, notably its horses. A horse cost at least $110, or ten times the monthly pay of a private soldier and five

times the price of a rifle musket. On top of this the cavalry[man] would require a saddle, a saber, riding boots, a few pistols (preferably the latest Colts), not to mention horseshoes and tack [i.e., saddle and bridle]. The whole proposition was so disproportionately complicated, when compared with the simple needs of an infantryman, that it is scarcely surprising that so few cavalry regiments were put into the field.

made up a division; and two to three divisions made up a corps. Accompanying this organization was an increasing tendency to use large units of horsemen, at times numbering as many as twelve thousand at once, as mobile offensive forces.

By contrast, a typical Confederate cavalry regiment had ten squadrons of roughly seventy to ninety-five men each, including officers. Like a Northern troop, a Southern squadron was commanded by a captain. Two to six Confederate cavalry regiments made up a brigade, and four to six brigades made up a division. As the war dragged on, these units became increasingly undermanned and therefore weaker and less reliable.

Lifting the Fog of War

The various cavalry units of both sides had numerous duties and tasks to perform. The most important was gathering and conveying vital military information. Despite some intelligence provided by spies, commanders were often unsure of enemy troop strengths and movements, even when the enemy was located nearby. "Civil War generals conducted their operations in a perpetual state of uncertainty," Ian Drury remarks. "The 'fog of war' was an inescapable part of military operations."[40] To help lift this fog as much as possible, commanders relied on their mobile and swift horsemen to scout enemy forces and report back.

A classic example occurred in early summer 1862. General Lee was worried about a Union army led by General George McClellan that was threatening the Confederate capital of Richmond. To acquire information about the numbers and positions of McClellan's troops, Lee sent a large cavalry unit led by J.E.B. Stuart to ride around the enemy's flank and rear. As noted Civil War scholar James McPherson tells it,

> With 1,200 picked men he [Stuart] rode north from Richmond on June 12 and swung east . . . brushing aside the small enemy patrols he encountered. Stuart's progress was helped by the fragmented organization of the Union cavalry, which was sprinkled by . . . regiments throughout the army instead of consolidated into a separate division as the southern cavalry was. Stuart's troopers discovered the location of [Union commander] Fitz-John Porter's 5th [Infantry] Corps, which McClellan had kept north of the Chickahominy [River] while transferring the rest of the army to the other side. Stuart had accomplished his mission. But he knew that by now the enemy was swarming in his rear. . . . He pushed on, winning skirmishes, capturing 170 enemy soldiers and nearly twice as many horses and mules, [and] destroying wagonloads of Union supplies. . . . Stuart's horsemen evaded further clashes and completed the circuit to Richmond by June 16, four days and a hundred miles after setting out.[41]

Raiding the Enemy's Heartland

While gathering crucial information, Stuart and his horsemen had also performed the second most important function of cavalry in the war—disrupting the enemy's commu-

Confederate cavalry commander Jeb Stuart leads his men on a mission to disrupt enemy supply lines and communications.

nications, supply lines, and way of life. Such activity was generally referred to as raiding. Stuart himself became famous for his successful raids. But it was the Union cavalry, as it gained in strength and efficiency in the later years of the war, that conducted the conflict's largest and most devastating raids.

The first major and successful Northern cavalry raid, one of the most spectacular of the war, occurred in May 1863 during General Grant's Vicksburg campaign. Gaining control of Vicksburg (in western Mississippi) would give the Union control of the Mississippi River. But to help accomplish this goal, Grant needed a way to distract the Confederates while his army crossed the

river. To this end, he ordered Colonel Benjamin H. Grierson to lead a cavalry raid into central Mississippi and create as much havoc as possible. Grierson departed La Grange, Tennessee, with seventeen hundred horsemen and cut a bold six-hundred-mile-long path southward through the heart of Mississippi. In his detailed report of the operation, he later described his passage through the town of Decatur:

> Lieutenant-Colonel Blackburn dashed into the town, took possession of the railroad and telegraph, and succeeded in capturing two trains in less than half an hour after his arrival. One of these,

GRIERSON'S CAVALRY IN A SOUTHERN TOWN

In his report describing his successful raid through Mississippi (quoted in Henry Commager's The Blue and the Gray), *Union cavalry commander Benjamin Grierson told how not all of the Southerners he encountered were enthusiastic supporters of the Confederate cause.*

After resting about three hours, we moved south to Garlandville. At this point we found the citizens, many of them venerable with age, armed with shot-guns and organized to resist our approach. As the advance [guard of horsemen] entered the town, these citizens fired upon them and wounded one of our men. We charged upon them and captured several. After disarming them, we showed them the folly of their actions and released them. Without an exception they acknowledged their mistake, and declared that they had been grossly deceived as to our real character. One volunteered his services as guide, and upon leaving us declared that hereafter his prayers should be for the Union Army. I mention this as a sample of the feeling which exists, and the good effect which our presence produced among the people in the country through which we passed. Hun-

dreds who are skulking and hiding out to avoid conscription, only await the presence of our arms to sustain them, when they will rise up and declare their principles; and thousands who have been deceived, upon the vindication of our cause would immediately return to loyalty [to the Union].

Colonel Benjamin H. Grierson, who led a huge Union cavalry raid through Mississippi.

[with] 25 cars, was loaded with [railroad] ties and machinery, and the other 13 cars were loaded with commissary stores and ammunition, among the latter several thousand loaded shells. These, together with a large quantity of commissary and quartermaster's stores and about five hundred stand of arms stored in the town, were destroyed. Seventy-five prisoners captured at this point were paroled. The

locomotives were exploded and otherwise rendered completely unserviceable. Here the track was torn up, and a bridge half a mile west of the station destroyed. I detached a battalion . . . under Major Starr to proceed eastward and destroy such bridges, etc., as he might find over the Chunkey River. [42]

Summing up the expedition's overall accomplishments, Grierson wrote:

We killed and wounded about 100 of the enemy, captured and paroled over 500 prisoners, many of them officers, destroyed between 50 and 60 miles of railroad and telegraph, captured and destroyed over 3,000 stand of arms, and other army stores and government property of an immense amount; we also captured 1,000 horses and mules. Our loss during the entire journey was 3 killed, 7 wounded . . . and 9 men missing. . . . We marched over 600 miles in sixteen days.[43]

Grierson's raid did more than achieve its primary goal of diverting the Confederates' attention from Grant's approach to Vicksburg. The expedition also spread fear throughout the South and showed other Union generals that cavalry could be a powerful military tool. Other Union cavalry raids ensued, culminating in the largest of the war. Early in 1865, a daring young commander named James H. Wilson led more than twelve thousand horsemen into the heart of Alabama. They destroyed huge numbers of railroads, bridges, cotton fields, factories, and arsenals and captured the city of Montgomery, spreading panic among the locals.

Cavalry on the March

When on the march, units of horsemen like those led by Wilson, Grierson, and Stuart could easily cover as many as thirty-five miles in an eight-hour day. But much longer

One common raiding tactic was the crippling of railroads. Here, wooden ties have been piled up in preparation for burning. The heat of the fire will bend the iron rails on top.

distances were possible when need dictated. When Stuart raided Chambersburg, Pennsylvania, in 1862, he drove his horsemen some eighty miles in only twenty-seven hours. In such conditions, the riders had no choice but to attempt to get at least some sleep in the saddle. One Southern trooper later recalled,

> There was no place to lie down and to stand in the snow only aggravated the discomfort. But when mounted, the men would pull the capes of their overcoats over their heads, drop their chins upon their breasts, and sleep. The horses plodded along and doubtless were asleep too, doing their work as a somnambulist [sleepwalker] might.[44]

Troopers on the march also traveled as light as possible, since overloading one's mount was sure to have negative results. This was especially true during large lightning raids into enemy territory, where speed and maneuverability were essential. In their great excursion through Alabama, for example, each of Wilson's horsemen carried just five days' worth of light rations, one hundred rounds of ammunition, twenty-four pounds of grain (for his horse), and two extra horseshoes. Extra food and ammunition, along with all other essential materials, were carried in a supply train made up of about 250 wagons.

Needless to say, keeping a cavalry army like Wilson's on the move was a major logistical undertaking. Part of the challenge was maintaining the good organization and strict discipline needed to keep such a large unit of horsemen from disintegrating into many smaller and more vulnerable units. Consider such an army stretched out along a road. A troop of ninety-six horsemen riding in a column four abreast was about ninety-five yards long. And many roads at the time could accommodate only two or three horses abreast. At times, Wilson's twelve thousand men and 250 wagons formed a column that stretched for almost twenty miles. Yet he was able to keep them together as a cohesive unit during the whole mission.

Charges on Infantry

In addition to marching, gathering intelligence, and raiding, Civil War cavalry units fought in pitched battles, although their participation in such fights was relatively infrequent and small-scale. Usually only a few hundred horsemen took part, supporting thousands and on occasion tens of thousands of foot soldiers. Of the 12,500 Union soldiers who died at Fredericksburg in December 1862, for example, only eight were cavalrymen. And in the first three years of the war, Northern cavalry made only five charges on infantry during the course of major battles. The saber, the sword of choice for mounted troops, was used only occasionally; carbines and pistols became the most common cavalry weapons.

By comparison, in a typical large battle during the Napoleonic Wars, thousands of horsemen fought; four or five charges on infantry might occur in only two or three hours; and the saber was the primary cavalry weapon. Thus, in the Civil War, the Americans broke sharply with the traditional cavalry tactics that had been used in Europe for centuries. One reason was that the United States had no long-standing, entrenched cavalry tradition like that of Eu-

A unit of Union cavalry charges onrushing Confederates near Brandy Station, in northern Virginia. Full-scale cavalry charges on infantry were rare in the Civil War.

rope, which dated back to the knights of medieval times. More important, the Americans of the 1860s had rifled muskets. With their long range and accuracy, these weapons could decimate a large mass of charging horsemen.

The few exceptions, when cavalry charges on infantry did occur during the Civil War, generally proved that this tactic had become outmoded. At Gaines' Mill, Virginia, in June 1862, more than 250 Union horsemen attacked the Confederate foot soldiers, but the charge failed to make any significant headway and the horsemen suffered 150 casualties. At the great Battle of Gettysburg, in July 1863, the North's 1st West Virginia and 1st Vermont cavalry units charged the right flank of the Confederate army, but the Southern foot soldiers easily repulsed these attacks. "Although certain positive results could possibly be claimed for each charge," Paddy Griffith states,

the overall outcome can only be described as very negative indeed. This finding would seem to suggest that the day of the cavalry charge had passed; that the rifle musket's improved firepower had given a new security to infantry . . . and that the American cavalry had really been rather wise not to charge more frequently in these battles than it did, in view of the probable outcome.[45]

Fighting on Foot

In fact, while mounted charges remained rare, most of the actual fighting done by cavalry in the war was accomplished on foot. Often, both Confederate and Union cavalry dismounted to fight, partly because it was easier to load and fire their weapons when they did not have to control their horses at the same time. But there were other reasons for dismounting as well: to capture and hold ground until the infantry arrived; to fill gaps in a line of foot soldiers at the height of a battle; or to attack an enemy position in a place where horses could not maneuver. As one Confederate cavalry officer said in comparing fighting on horseback to fighting on foot,

The latter method was much oftener practiced—we were in fact not cavalry, but mounted riflemen. A small body of mounted men was usually kept in reserve to act on the flanks [of the infantry], cover the retreat [of the infantry] or press a victory, but otherwise our men fought very little on horseback, except on scouting expeditions.[46]

BUFORD'S HORSEMEN HOLD THE FIELD

Cavalry played an important role in the opening of the most famous battle of the Civil War, the Battle of Gettysburg (in southern Pennsylvania) in early July 1863. Cavalry commander John Buford and his men dismounted and took up positions behind rocks and trees; from there, they held the field against three times as many Confederate infantrymen while waiting for Union reinforcements to arrive. A Union major, Joseph Rosengarten, later commented (in a newspaper account quoted in Henry Commager's The Blue and the Gray):

The brilliant achievement of Buford, with his small body of cavalry, up to that time hardly appreciated as to the right use to be made of them, is but too little considered in the history of the battle of Gettysburg. It was his foresight and energy, his pluck and self-reliance, in thrusting forward his forces and pushing the enemy, and thus inviting, almost compelling their return, that brought on the engagement of the first of July.

Union cavalry commander John Buford played a key role in the fight at Gettysburg.

(Dismounting to fight remained a common cavalry tactic in the years immediately following the war; General George Armstrong Custer, a distinguished Civil War cavalry commander, ordered his men to dismount at the Battle of the Little Big Horn, fought between the U.S. 7th Cavalry and Sioux Indians in 1876.)

In those situations in which cavalry dismounted, it was customary for one out of every four men to hold the horses while the others fought. This reduced the unit's firepower by 25 percent. But the Union cavalry more than made up for this loss when it issued its horsemen quick-loading Sharps and Spencer carbines late in the war. Indeed, had the Northern cavalry been as well armed, well organized, and formidable at the start of the war as it was at the end, the conflict might have been considerably shorter.

CHAPTER FIVE

Ships and Naval Warfare

From a naval standpoint, both sides in the American Civil War began woefully unprepared. Seldom has a war leader at the start of a major conflict faced so daunting a challenge as the Union's secretary of the navy,

Gideon Welles, the Union's skilled and hardworking secretary of the navy.

Gideon Welles. He had only about ninety vessels. And fifty of them were sailing ships that had become nearly obsolete in the wake of recent advances in steam-powered ships. (The first American steam-powered warship, the *Princeton,* had been built in 1842.) Moreover, most of the forty steamships in the U.S. fleet were in foreign ports or on duty in distant seas. Only twelve were available for immediate use in American waters. Welles's roster of naval officers and seamen was also inadequate. He had only about twelve hundred officers, most of whom had either never seen military action or were too old to serve (there was no effective retirement system yet for naval officers), and fewer than seventy-five hundred seamen. This small force of ships and men was suddenly expected to patrol an enemy coastline more than three thousand miles long.

Desperate, Welles put out the call for existing vessels of any kind. He also ordered Union shipyards to begin a crash building program. In an amazingly short amount of time, the U.S. Navy grew into a force to be reckoned with. The credit belongs mainly to the capable and tireless Welles. As Jack Coggins says, he "was the right man in the right job. And it was due in great measure to his energy and foresight . . . that at the war's end over five hundred armed vessels flew the Stars and Stripes."[47]

The Confederacy faced an even worse situation when the war began. "It had no navy," historian Henry S. Commager writes,

and no naval personnel except such as had resigned from the Union Navy at the outbreak of the war. Both its navy yards fell to the Union before the end of the war. Yet somehow it managed to create a navy. It captured

some ships, built others, raised several that had been sunk at Norfolk [in Virginia], converted a few merchant ships into warships, fitted out privateers [privately owned armed vessels], [and] bought and built vessels abroad.[48]

Thanks to ingenuity and hard work, both sides ended up with an almost bewildering variety of warships. In addition to merchant ships, other nonmilitary vessels converted for military use included whalers, riverboats, harbor tugs, fishing schooners, ferryboats, and private yachts. These and the ones built from scratch fought mostly on rivers and in bays but also occasionally on

The warship Merrimack, *which had been sunk at the Gosport Navy Yard in Norfolk, Virginia, is remodeled into a Confederate ironclad ship late in 1861.*

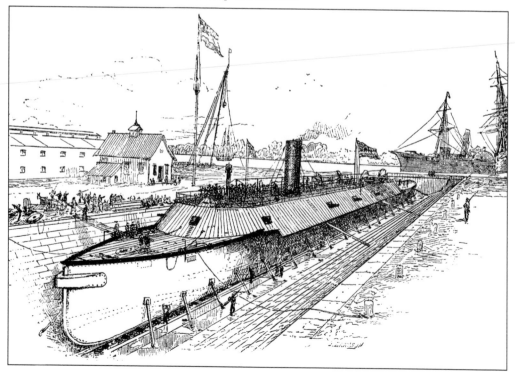

the high seas. Their use followed a few basic and broad strategies. The Union sought
first to blockade Southern ports in hopes of
reducing the South's volume of trade and
thereby damaging its economy. The North
also wanted to gain control of the major
rivers, especially the Mississippi. That
would cut off Texas and Arkansas from the
rest of the Confederacy and allow Northern
soldiers and supplies to move rapidly to
strategic locations. Meanwhile, the South
wanted to evade the blockade any way it
could while presenting a credible defense
against attacks by Union ships.

An Economic Weapon: The Blockade

Both the imposition and evasion of the
blockade were immense and dangerous un-
dertakings. President Lincoln created the
blockade by issuing two proclamations in
April 1861. The blockade extended from
Chesapeake Bay in Virginia to the Rio
Grande in Texas and encompassed about a
dozen major ports and nearly two hundred
minor ones. It was almost an impossible task
to stop at least some blockade runners—ships
attempting to penetrate the blockade—from
getting through. The following recollection

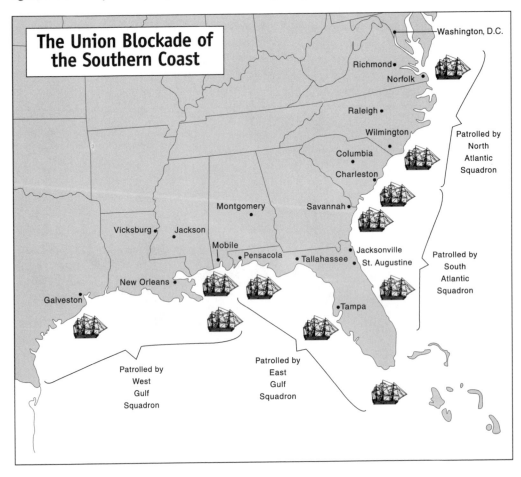

The Union Blockade of the Southern Coast

Washington, D.C.

Richmond
Norfolk

Raleigh

Wilmington

Columbia
Charleston

Patrolled by North Atlantic Squadron

Montgomery   Savannah

Vicksburg   Jackson

Mobile
Pensacola   Tallahassee   Jacksonville
St. Augustine

New Orleans

Patrolled by South Atlantic Squadron

Galveston

Tampa

Patrolled by West Gulf Squadron

Patrolled by East Gulf Squadron

Three steamships, the Neptune, Vesta, *and* Alliance, *prepare to attempt a run on the Union blockade.*

by Horatio Wait, a Union naval paymaster, gives some idea of the enormity of the challenge:

> How was it possible to undertake such a blockade as this, along such a vast extent of coast, when so few ships of any kind were available? . . . The service to be performed by [the wide range of vessel types being assembled] was as unique as the fleet itself. The entire outer coast of the Confederacy was 3,549 miles in extent. . . . To guard the ordinary entrances to [the large] ports was comparatively a simple task. There was, however, a greater difficulty to be met; for the outer coastline is only the exterior edge of a series of islands between which and the mainland there is an elaborate network of navigable sounds and passages, having numerous inlets communicating with the sea. . . . As soon as we closed a

port, by stationing vessels at the main entrance . . . the blockade runners would slip in at some of the numerous remote inlets, reaching their destination by the inside passages; so that blockade-running flourished until we were able to procure as many blockaders as there were channels and inlets to be guarded. [49]

The ships that tried to run the blockade fell into four basic categories: those owned by the Confederate government; those financed by state governments; those owned by private individuals; and foreign vessels either sympathetic to the Confederate cause or seeking to profit from it. Historians estimate that at least six hundred ships acted as runners during the war and that they violated the blockade at least eight thousand times. Only a partial list of the goods they smuggled in included 600,000 firearms, 550,000 pairs of shoes, and large amounts of metals, cloth, leather, and foodstuffs. To

Among the more effective naval cannons was the Dahlgren gun, sometimes called the "soda bottle" gun because of its distinct shape.

make as much space as possible for this contraband and keep the vessels light and fast, the blockade runners carried no cannons or other large weapons. The ships depended not only on speed but on stealth. They often traveled at night, burned types of coal that gave off little smoke, and flew phony flags, including the Stars and Stripes.

At first these tactics met with considerable success. In 1861, when Union efforts to impose the blockade were still spotty and inefficient, chances of capture were only one in ten. But these odds narrowed in direct proportion to the increasing numbers of Northern blockaders and patrols. By 1864, the chances of a runner being captured were one in three, and after January 1865, blockade running diminished to a mere trickle.

"What all this adds up to," Commager says, "is that the blockade was a decisive factor in the Union victory. We cannot say that without it the Confederacy would have won, but it is clear that without it the war would have been greatly prolonged and might have ended in a stalemate." [50]

Armor: The Wave of the Future?

While the blockaders and blockade runners faced off in one major theater of the naval war, other ships attempted to attack or defend strategic positions or simply intimidate the enemy and drain his resources. The nature of many of the sea battles of the Civil War was different than in most of those of the past. This was because the conflict occurred at a time when warships and naval war tactics were in a state of rapid change and modernization. Some old-fashioned sailing ships were still in use, but they were quickly being replaced by more maneuverable and reliable steam-powered vessels. Moreover, many of the cannons carried by warships in the 1860s were much larger and more powerful than those used in the War of 1812 and Napoleonic Wars.

Of particular note were Dahlgren guns, named after their inventor, U.S. Navy lieutenant John A. Dahlgren. Beginning in the late 1840s, he developed very large smoothbore naval cannons in calibers ranging from nine to thirteen inches. The weapons were not only extremely powerful but could fire large explosive shells as well as solid shot.

Dahlgren and other weapons experts saw that shells were the wave of the future in naval warfare. The chilling proof of this reality was demonstrated in 1853 when six Russian battleships fired explosive shells at a Turkish fleet of traditional wooden warships in a battle in the Black Sea; the entire Turkish fleet burned and sank, and most of its sailors died.

It began to dawn on Russian, British, French, and American naval planners that the only effective way to deal with the growing threat of naval shells was to phase out wooden ships and build new ones with metal armor. However, the actual implementation of such plans was slow to materialize, as illustrated by the American experience. As early as 1842, the U.S. Navy

The 512-ton Union ironclad river gunboat Baron De Kalb *fought with distinction in Arkansas before being sunk by a Confederate mine in July 1863.*

had authorized a visionary named Robert L. Stevens to build an experimental "ironclad" steamship of his own design. Unfortunately, the vessel was still unfinished when Stevens died in 1856. (It was never completed.) And Congress, which clearly did not anticipate the outbreak of an American civil conflict or any other war, dragged its feet and ordered no other ironclads until 1861.

Late in that year, the Confederate naval secretary, Stephen Mallory, set the American naval arms race in motion. He hoped to make his forces superior to those of the Union by building an ironclad (with plans to build more eventually). A former Union wooden warship, the *Merrimack,* which had been badly damaged in a fire at Norfolk, Virginia, in April 1861, had fallen into Confederate hands. Mallory ordered his engineers to transform the vessel into an ironclad. They covered its 270-foot-long hull with more than eight hundred tons of iron plates, many of them two inches thick. They also outfitted the ship with a 2,500-pound iron ram in its bow and ten heavy, powerful cannons. Finally, they renamed the vessel the *Virginia,* although most people still continued to call it the *Merrimack.*

In the North, meanwhile, Gideon Welles was pressing Congress for funds to build ironclads for the Union. Ominous reports of the refitting of the *Merrimack* worried many people in the North and strengthened Welles's argument that the U.S. Navy also needed to produce armor-plated warships. Of the three designs accepted by the navy, two were for conventional wooden vessels with armor plating added, like the *Merrimack;* the third was for a warship fabricated almost entirely from metal. The third design, by naval engineer John Ericsson, resulted in the *Monitor,* commissioned on February 25,

The 1,006-ton Confederate ironclad ram Atlanta, *pictured here, ran aground in battle and was captured. It subsequently became a Union warship.*

The ironclad Merrimack *(or* CSS Virginia*) plows into and sinks the* USS Cumberland *in the great naval battle off Hampton Roads.*

1862. Its length was 172 feet, making it considerably smaller than the *Merrimack*. One of the *Monitor*'s advantages was that it sat very low in the water, offering only a small proportion of its hull as a target; it also boasted a revolving gun turret protected by iron armor eleven inches thick.

The Fateful Battles at Hampton Roads

The two ironclads seemed destined to come to grips in open battle. In the words of historian Bern Anderson,

> Early in 1862 tension on both sides increased as both *Merrimack* and

Monitor neared completion. So great was the pressure [by Southern war leaders] to get *Merrimack* into action before *Monitor* appeared that when she got under way for the first time on March 8, her crew thought she was merely going on a trial run. [51]

It was no trial run, however. The *Merrimack*'s captain, Franklin Buchanan, took the ship to Hampton Roads, Virginia, at a strategic point in Chesapeake Bay and brazenly attacked several Union warships. The first to suffer was the USS *Cumberland*. Its nine-inch Dahlgren guns blazed away at the attacking ironclad but to little or

BATTLE OF THE IRONCLADS

In a March 14, 1862, letter to his parents (printed in Lydia M. Post's Soldiers' Letters from Camp, Battlefield, and Prison*), S.D. Greene, an officer on the* Monitor, *described the furious battle between that ironclad and its Confederate rival, the* Merrimack.

After the first gun was fired we forgot all fatigues, hard work, and everything else and fought as hard as men ever fought. We loaded and fired as fast as we could. I pointed and fired the guns myself. Every shot I would ask the captain the effect, and the majority of them were encouraging. The captain was in the pilothouse, directing the movements of the vessel. . . . Five times during the engagement we touched each other, and each time I fired a gun at her. . . . Once she tried to run us down with her iron prow but did no damage whatever. After fighting for two hours we hauled off for half an hour to hoist shot in the tower. At it we went again as hard as we could, the shot, shell, grape, canister, musket, and rifle balls flying in every direction but doing no damage. Our tower was struck several times, and though the noise was pretty loud it did not affect us any. . . . At about 11:30 A.M. the captain sent for me. I went forward, and there stood as noble a man as lives, at the foot of the ladder to the pilothouse, his face perfectly black with powder and iron, and apparently perfectly blind. I asked him what was the matter. He said a shot had struck the pilothouse exactly opposite his eye and blinded him, and he thought the pilothouse was damaged. He told me to take charge of the ship and use my own discretion.

no effect. The *Merrimack* picked up a burst of speed and rammed the other vessel, which soon sank. Next, the *Merrimack* chased down and shelled the USS *Congress,* which burst into flames and several hours later exploded when the fire reached the ammunition storage. Buchanan's ironclad also attacked and damaged the USS *Minnesota* before leaving the scene.

Early the next morning, the *Merrimack* returned to finish off the hapless *Minnesota.* But by this time the Union's own fearsome ironclad, the *Monitor,* was on the scene. The two vessels closed in on each other, and for more than four hours, the world's first battle between metal-armored warships raged as thousands of people watched from nearby shores. The shorter, lighter *Monitor* was consistently able to outmaneuver its opponent; however, no matter how hard they tried, neither vessel could significantly damage the other. This was astonishing considering that both frequently came close and fired at point-blank range. Lieutenant S.D. Greene, second in command of the *Monitor,* later recalled,

Five times during the engagement we touched each other, and each time I fired a gun at her. . . . Once she tried to run us down with her iron prow but did no damage whatever. . . . [We attacked her] as hard as we could, the shot, shell, grape, canister, musket, and rifle balls flying in every direction but doing no damage. Our tower was struck several times . . . [but] it did not affect us any. [52]

The battles at Hampton Roads showed clearly that the future of naval warfare belonged to armor-plated ships. But the fight between the *Merrimack* and *Monitor* also revealed the existing limitations of ironclads. Their guns were still not very accurate and took a long time to load; also, their shells, though deadly to wooden ships, were not very effective against the armor of other ironclads. According to Ian Drury (who here refers to the *Merrimack* by its other name, the *Virginia*),

When *Virginia* was examined after the two-day battle, she had been struck 97 times. [There was] evidence of 20 hits from *Monitor*'s guns. *Monitor* had fired 55 times during the battle, taking 6–8 minutes to reload her guns. . . . *Virginia*'s shooting was less accurate, partly because the gunners were aiming at a smaller target and they had been ordered to concentrate on the little pilot house near the bow. Exactly how many rounds she fired is unknown, but she had ten guns to *Monitor*'s two and the 9-inch Dahlgrens were certainly faster to load. She scored 24 hits on her opponent; the pilot house was hit, blinding *Monitor*'s captain, and hits on the turret sent bolts flying around the interior. As *Monitor* was hampered by having to use half charges for her guns, so *Virginia* was frustrated by running out of solid shot. Almost all the projectiles she fired at the Union

ironclad were shells, which were less effective against an armored target. . . . It was unusual for a Civil War ironclad's armor to be penetrated by shot or shell. [53]

Rams and Subs

The advent of the steam-powered ironclads, which were able to maneuver without the power of the winds, showed that the old naval tactics of sail-powered warships were a thing of the past. Yet ironclads were not the only vessels to take advantage of the new tactics in the Civil War. Some clever naval engineers realized that ordinary steamers, if fast enough and outfitted with sturdy rams in their bows, could sink ships simply by ramming them; such "rams," as these vessels came to be called, might even be able to puncture and sink the formidable ironclad *Merrimack*.

To that end, early in 1862 Union engineer Charles Ellet, of Pittsburgh, bought nine fast steamers and fitted each with a reinforced bow. His little fleet of rams quickly made its way down the Mississippi to aid several Union gunboats (small river craft outfitted with cannons) in an assault on the Confederate city of Memphis, Tennessee. In a tremendous battle fought near the city on June 6, Ellet's rams, which carried no weapons except their rams, proved their worth. All but one of the Confederate gunboats, many of which had armor plating, were destroyed or captured. Ellet himself was wounded in the fight and died soon afterward, leaving his brother Alfred to comment:

The battle of Memphis was, in many respects, one of the most remarkable naval victories on record. For [our] unarmed, frail, wooden river steamboats, with barely men enough on board to handle the machinery and keep the furnace-fires burning, to rush to the front, between two hostile fleets, and *into* the enemy's advancing line . . . was a sight never before witnessed.[54]

Still another mechanical innovation applied to naval warfare during the conflict was the submarine (or submersible). A few crude experiments with subs had occurred as early as the American Revolution, but none produced weapons of any credible destructive power until the Civil War. In submarine warfare, despite its lack of industrial capacity (or perhaps because of it, which stimulated innovation), the South led the way.

The first attempt to use below-the-waterline attack craft was inspired by a need to deliver a "spar torpedo." Invented by a young Charleston engineer, Francis D. Lee, a spar torpedo was a can of gunpowder attached to a long spar, or pole. The South created a new class of warships with spar torpedoes extending forward from their bows; because a small part of each ship remained above water, they were semisubmersibles rather than

Charles Ellet's steam rams charge and destroy a fleet of Confederate gunboats in the Battle of Memphis on June 6, 1862.

ELLET'S STEAM RAMS ON THE ATTACK

This recollection of the Battle of Memphis (quoted in Henry Commager's The Blue and the Gray) *is by Alfred W. Ellet, brother of Colonel Charles Ellet, the inventor of the Union steam rams.*

When freed from the smoke, those of us who were on the *Monarch* [Ellet's lead ship], could see Colonel Ellet's tall and commanding form still standing on the hurricane-deck, waving his hat to show me which one of the enemy's vessels he desired the *Monarch* to attack,—namely, the *General Price,* which was on the right wing of their advancing line. For himself he selected the *General Lovell* and directed the *Queen* straight for her, she being about the middle of the enemy's advancing line. The two vessels came toward each other in most gallant style, head to head, prow to prow; and had they met in that way, it is most likely that both vessels would have gone down. But at the critical moment the *General Lovell* began to turn; and that moment sealed her fate. The *Queen* came on and plunged straight into the *Lovell's* exposed broadside; the vessel was cut almost in two and disappeared under the dark waters in less time than it takes to tell the story. The *Monarch* next struck the *General Price* a glancing blow which cut her starboard wheel clean off, and completely disabled her from further participation in the fight. As soon as the *Queen* was freed from the wreck of the sinking *Lovell,* and before she could recover headway, she was attacked on both sides by the enemy's vessels, the *Beauregard* on one side and the *Sumter* on the other. In the mêlée one of the wheels of the *Queen* was disabled so that she could not use it, and Colonel Ellet, while still standing on the hurricane-deck to view the encounter with the *General Lovell,* received a pistol ball in his knee. . . . Colonel Ellet sent an officer and squad of men to meet the *General Price* upon her making the shore, and received her entire crew as prisoners of war. By this time consternation had seized upon the enemy's fleet, and all had turned to escape.

true submarines. As Anderson describes them,

These were cigar-shaped vessels fifty-four feet long and five and one half feet in diameter, powered by a steam engine. They were heavily ballasted to ride low in the water and had an open cockpit about twelve feet long in the center, in which rode the eight-man crew. At the end of a ten-foot rod attached to the bow was a spar torpedo with a seventy-pound charge of powder and an ingenious exploder. The first one was named *David* and that name was retained for others that were built.[55]

The first true submarine constructed by the Confederacy was the *Hunley,* the namesake of its builder, Captain Horace L. Hunley. It was made from an iron boiler twenty feet long and five feet wide. Eight or nine crewmen working in a very cramped space turned a metal shaft that spun the propeller. On the night of February 17, 1864, the *Hunley* delivered a spar torpedo to the hull of the USS *Housatonic* near Charleston

The Confederate Hunley *was the first submarine in history to sink an enemy ship in battle. The blast destroyed the* USS Housatonic *and also badly damaged the sub.*

and destroyed it, becoming the first submarine in history to sink a ship. However, the blast also wrecked the sub, ending its career on the same day it had started.

Toward the end of the war, the North also experimented with submarines. But the conflict ended before they or other Southern ones saw service. Instead, the experiments with the Davids and submersibles foreshadowed a new and devastating kind of naval weaponry that would become a major factor in future wars.

CHAPTER SIX

Espionage and Experimental Weapons

W hen the American Civil War is mentioned, the popular imagination most often conjures up long lines of soldiers clad in blue and gray marching toward and firing at each other, or ironclad warships vainly attempting to penetrate each other's hulls. These are the familiar overt, visible manifestations of the war. Yet they tell only part of the story of this remarkable conflict. There was also a much less visible aspect—what might be called a secret war. It included espionage (spying) and the development of new, often strange weapons, some of which were designed to terrorize the enemy.

The Potential of Espionage

The goal of espionage is to gather military intelligence, vital information about one's enemy that might be used to defeat him or her. The sad state of the intelligence-gathering abilities of both sides at the start of the war is a testament to how often people forget the lessons of history. Spying had played an important role in the American defeat of Britain in the American Revolu-

tion; George Washington and other American leaders relied heavily on and greatly benefited from information supplied by well-organized spy networks and individual spies. Yet in the decades following the American victory, the country largely forgot this chapter of the Revolution. Virtually no organized espionage took place in the War of 1812. And when the Civil War broke out, no one had any clear notion of how such activities might be organized and exploited. Edwin C. Fishel, an authority on Civil War espionage, writes:

> It would be difficult to imagine a nation entering a war more unprepared to obtain information about its enemy than the United States of 1861. In the almost ludicrously small U.S. Army there was no intelligence staff, no corps of spies, trained or otherwise. There was not so much as a concept on which a plan for these services could be based. If, hidden away in some file of regulations,

there was even one paragraph for the guidance of a commander with an intelligence problem to solve, it was for all practical purposes unknown in 1861, and its obscurity was preserved throughout the war.[56]

Despite the lack of professional intelligence-gathering capabilities at the beginning of the war, both sides quickly recognized the potential of spying. And there was no shortage of Northerners and Southerners who were ready to spy for their respective sides. At least at first, Confederate spies enjoyed some distinct advantages over their Union counterparts. (As time went on, however, the North gained considerable sophistication in the realm of espionage, and in the conflict's last years its spies were consistently more successful.) To begin with, the Union had an organized, functioning government for Southerners to spy on; by contrast,

the Confederacy's government was just getting started. Also, numerous high-ranking Confederates in that new government had recently been high-ranking officials in the federal government, so many of them already possessed vital information that could be used against the Union.

Moreover, not everyone who supported the Confederate cause left Washington, D.C. "There were Confederate sympathizers in positions of trust in the U.S. government at the beginning of the war," scholar Donald Markle points out, "and many of them, particularly the ones strategically placed, were convinced they should stay in those positions during the entire conflict. . . . The Union could not duplicate this in the early stages of the Confederacy."[57]

Spies in Petticoats
Whenever they could, these highly placed Confederate sympathizers passed on infor-

 # ROSE'S EXPLOITS EXAGGERATED?

Edwin C. Fishel, an authority on Civil War espionage contends that the importance of "Rebel Rose" Greenhow's spy exploits are in large degree overblown. She was arrogant, he says, and sloppy, often leaving compromising written documents in plain sight in her home, where Union agents found them. Also, she exaggerated her own deeds in her memoirs, which became popular reading after the war. In his Secret War for the Union, *Fishel writes:*

Rose Greenhow soon became a Confederate heroine. It would seem that the Southern gratitude she had received is more than she deserves. From the quality of her reports it is

clear that she was no great success at garnering information. Whatever adulation she is entitled to must be for her tremendous courage and drive and her apparent ability to draw collaborators, some of them perhaps unwitting, into her net. A more serious failing was her irrational and arrogant underrating of the "Black Republican dogs" [Union officials]. Such was her contempt for them that she became foolishly careless, as shown by the evidence of espionage that she kept about her premises. With different emotional equipment she could have continued spying for a long time, perhaps as long as the war lasted.

Confederate spy Rose O'Neal Greenhow, better known as "Rebel Rose," poses with her daughter in a Union prison courtyard.

mation to spies, who either carried it south themselves or handed it off to secret couriers. Many of these spies were women. In fact, never before or since have women played so large a part in American espionage efforts. Perhaps the most famous of these so-called spies in petticoats was Rose O'Neal Greenhow, who eventually became known to millions as "Rebel Rose." Her husband, a prominent member of the U.S. State Department, died in 1854. After his death, she continued to hobnob with high-ranking politicians and military leaders, including President James Buchanan (who served from 1857 to 1861).

When the Civil War broke out in April 1861, Greenhow decided to use her unique social position and valuable connections in Washington to aid the Confederacy. According to her later testimony, "I employed every capacity with which God has endowed me, and the result was far more successful than my hopes could have flattered me to expect."[58] As it turns out, she was not nearly as successful as she wanted people to believe. Her major claim to fame was supplying important information about Union troop movements to Confederate general P.G.T. Beauregard; this knowledge helped him defeat the Union forces at the first battle at Bull Run in July 1861. However, Greenhow was a consistently careless spy who was soon arrested by Union agents, and the importance of most of her secret activities was later exaggerated, most often by herself in her sensational memoirs, *My Imprisonment and the First Year of Abolition Rule at Washington.*

A much more careful and successful female spy was Elizabeth Van Lew, a native of Richmond, Virginia, the Confederate capital. After attending school in Philadelphia, she became an ardent abolitionist determined to rid the South of the blight of slavery. When the war began, Van Lew set up a spy operation in Richmond to aid the Union. One of her most effective tactics was to bring baskets of food, medicine, and books to Union prisoners in Richmond's Libby Prison. While in the facility, Van Lew collected information about Confederate troop movements from newly arrived Northern soldiers; using her feminine charm, she also managed to glean vital information from prison guards and even the facility's commander. She then mailed the information to Federal authorities, eventually devising a sophisticated code to conceal her work in case the letters were intercepted. In addition, she sent family servants with baskets of farm produce northward. In the baskets were chickens' eggs, some of which contained encoded messages. Sometimes Van Lew sent intelligence directly to Ulysses S. Grant, who later claimed that her information was the most valuable he received during the war. Another Union general, George H. Sharpe, added this about her:

Libby Prison, in Richmond, Virginia, where master spy Elizabeth Van Lew gained vital information from Union prisoners.

For a long, long time she represented all that was left of the power of the U.S. government in Richmond. . . . The greatest portion of our intelligence in 1864–65 in its collection and in good measure in its transmission we owed to the intelligence and devotion of Elizabeth Van Lew.[59]

Another effective Union spy, Emma Edmonds, was one of several hundred women who managed to enlist in either the Union or Confederate army during the war. When the North began calling for soldiers, Edmonds cut her hair, donned men's clothes, assumed the name of Frank Thompson, and joined the ranks (recruits received no physical exam at the time). Soon she volunteered to become a spy for General George McClellan. To help fool the Confederates, Emma/Frank posed as a black slave by darkening her skin with silver nitrate and wearing a minstrel's wig. In that and other similar disguises, she repeatedly infiltrated enemy lines and then returned with valuable information. Later, she somewhat modestly said of her incredible triple life and espionage exploits, "I am naturally fond of adventure, a little ambitious, and a good deal romantic—but patriotism was the true secret of my success."[60]

Paid Spies and Zealous Saboteurs

Male spies, both Union and Confederate, also played their roles. President Lincoln himself recruited a New York businessman named William A. Lloyd to spy for the North. Lloyd, who published railroad and steamboat guides and maps of Southern states, wanted to obtain a pass through the

The ingenious and courageous Union spy Emma Edwards masquerades as a slave.

Union lines so he could continue his business ventures. Lincoln offered to grant passes to Lloyd and his associate, Thomas Boyd, providing that the men gathered whatever military intelligence they could while behind the lines. At first, Lloyd was reluctant. But then the president appealed to his business sense by offering him money. According to historian Alan Axelrod,

Whatever motives of patriotism Abraham Lincoln may have suggested to Lloyd . . . it was the offer of a two-hundred-dollar monthly salary that prompted the most serious thought from Lloyd. In an age when unskilled labor earned a dollar a day, two hundred dollars a month was inviting. . . . And it wasn't as if he had to do a lot of extra work to obtain the information Lincoln sought. Really, he just had to do what he had always done: collect timetables, study rail and shipping facilities, look into centers of transportation, [and] engage in conversation with his Southern business cronies. . . . He took the job.[61]

In the months and years that followed, Lloyd and Boyd collected and passed on to the North much valuable intelligence. Even after Lloyd was arrested and confined to a Confederate military barracks in Georgia, his small spy operation continued. He secretly received information from Boyd, who was still working on the outside. Lloyd then gave this information to captured Union soldiers who were about to be traded for Confederates held prisoner in the North; the soldiers carried the information northward.

One of the most active and colorful, if not always successful, of the Confederate male spies was Thomas H. Hines. Hines earned the nickname "the Fox" for his uncanny ability to evade Union pursuers or escape their clutches on those occasions when they did manage to capture him. When the war broke out, Hines enlisted and soon joined the famous Southern cavalry raiders led by John H. Morgan. Hines's espionage work, often directed by Morgan, started shortly afterward. It mostly involved attempts to sabotage Northern cities and states in an effort to bring those states into

Confederate cavalryman John H. Morgan, who directed some of Thomas Hines's spy activities.

the Confederate fold. In 1864, aides of Confederate president Jefferson Davis put Hines in charge of an audacious plan to murder the political leaders of several Northern states; overthrow the governments of these states; free all Confederate war prisoners held there; and burn Chicago and New York City.

Unfortunately for Hines, this plan, which came to be called the "Northwest Conspiracy," never came to fruition. Part of the problem was that the Confederacy did not commit enough men and resources to achieve such a large-scale objective; also, Hines, a well-meaning, zealous patriot, misjudged the enthusiasm of many of those he trusted to carry out the actual dirty work. However, as Markle points out, "The activities of Captain Hines and his group did cause concern in the Union and did require the detailing of valuable Union troops to counter his moves. In this sense he was successful."[62]

Spying from the Air

Aiding spies in the conventional ways of acquiring intelligence was an experimental device—the observation balloon. Balloons that could carry people were not new (car-nivals had featured them for many years), but the Civil War was the first conflict to employ them for aerial reconnaissance (gathering information from the air). Not surprisingly, it was a veteran balloonist who saw the method's potential. Not long after the war began, balloonist Thadeus Lowe approached Union general Winfield Scott with a proposal for creating a balloon corps for the Union army. After some brief consideration, the army agreed to finance seven experimental balloons.

Lowe's balloons worked by taking advantage of the fact that hydrogen gas is lighter than the gases that make up air; therefore, a balloon filled with hydrogen gas will rise into the air. Wagons carried

Thadeus Lowe (left) and one of his reconnaissance balloons being filled with hydrogen gas (below).

large boxlike generators to the desired spot. Inside the generators, sulfuric acid reacted with iron filings to produce the hydrogen, which a pressure regulator pumped into the balloons.

General McClellan took the balloons along on his expedition into southeastern Virginia in 1862. During the siege of Yorktown, Lowe deployed them, taking them up to heights of one thousand feet or more. (Long ropes were attached to keep them from drifting downwind.) From there, he and various Union officers, including George Armstrong Custer, Fitz-John Porter, and McClellan himself, scouted the surrounding terrain and observed enemy positions and movements. A colorful eyewitness account of one of Porter's adventures aloft, during which his balloon broke loose and drifted away, has survived:

The wayward canvas now turned due westward, and was blown rapidly toward the Confederate works. Its course was fitfully direct, and the wind seemed to veer often, as if contrary currents, conscious of the opportunity, were struggling for the possession of the daring navigator. The south wind held mastery for awhile, and the balloon passed the Federal front amid a howl of despair from the soldiery. It kept right on, over sharpshooters, rifle-pits, and outworks, and finally passed, as if to deliver up its freight, directly over the heights of Yorktown. The cool courage, either of heroism or despair, had seized upon Fitz John Porter. He turned his black [spy]glass upon the ramparts and masked cannon below, upon the remote camps, upon the beleaguered town, upon the guns of Gloucester Point, and upon distant Norfolk. Had he been reconnoitering from a secure perch at the tip of the

CONFEDERATE BALLOONS

In this excerpt from his Civil War Military Machine, *historian Ian Drury discusses Confederate efforts to gather military intelligence via balloon.*

The Confederates were not slow to appreciate the potential of observation balloons but they lacked the necessary facilities. Without the means to manufacture hydrogen gas, they hit upon a novel solution. A balloon was made at Richmond from silk dress material—a riotous patchwork of different colors and patterns. Inflated with town gas from the Richmond gas works, it was secured to a locomotive which steamed down the York River railroad to a suitable vantage point. The Confederate balloon provided useful intelligence . . . detecting and reporting the Union reinforcements crossing the Chickahominy during the battle of Gaines' Mill. After [Union general George] McClellan withdrew from Malvern Hill, the Confederates fixed the balloon to a little tug, the *Teaser*. Unfortunately for them, the tug ran hard aground on July 4, 1862, just as the tide fell. The crew escaped but Union troops captured the vessel and its bizarre cargo.

moon, he could not have been more vigilant, and the Confederates probably thought this some Yankee device to peer into their sanctuary in despite of ball or shell. None of their great guns of musketry appeared to have any effect, and finally even these demonstrations ceased. Both armies in solemn silence were gazing aloft, while the imperturbable [undisturbed] mariner continued to spy out the land.[63]

Metal Armor, Mines, and Machine Guns

Balloons were not the only new, seemingly strange weapons and devices experimented with by both sides in the war. Some manufacturers offered soldiers steel chest protectors—early versions of today's bulletproof vests—as well as metal leg armor. Such protection was often effective. One Union officer reported that he was hit by two bullets square in the chest and suffered no injury. Unfortunately, though, these outfits were very heavy, inflexible, and cumbersome. One Massachusetts artilleryman remarked of the men he saw wearing them: "These ironclad warriors admitted that when panoplied [armored] for the fight their sensations were much as they might be if they were dressed up in an old-fashioned air-tight stove."[64] Moreover, most soldiers teased and belittled the few men who did try wearing such outfits, calling them cowards. As a result, body armor saw little use during the conflict.

Unlike armor, a defensive device, most Civil War experimental weapons were offensive in nature. One used widely by the

This diagram shows how some Civil War torpedoes were held in place by weights.

Confederacy was the torpedo, which at the time was not a warhead fired by a ship (a later invention) but, rather, a mine that floated in the water. Water torpedoes were improvised from all sorts of metal containers. Most were simply filled with gunpowder and set adrift in areas where enemy ships were expected to pass. The outer surfaces of the mines were covered with pieces of fulminate or percussion caps, which, upon contact with ships' hulls, exploded the devices. Several Union ships were destroyed by torpedoes, including four Monitor-class ironclads.

Another version, the coal torpedo, did its damage from the inside rather than the outside of a ship. Basically, it was an irregular, hollow piece of metal painted black and covered with coal dust to make it look like a large lump of coal. Inside were several pounds of gunpowder. Confederate secret agents planted these torpedoes in Union coal piles, and when the devices eventually made their way into ships' boilers, explosions ensued. A number of strange boiler explosions on Union ships were probably caused by such weapons, which not only did damage but also spread fear and terror.

An experimental weapon that did less damage in the Civil War than the mine but considerably more damage in later wars was the machine gun. The destructive power of the Spencer rifle and other repeaters inspired some inventors to try to create guns that fired even more rapidly. By today's standards, the early machine guns were crude; in fact, it would be more accurate to call them mechanically operated repeaters, since they had to be cranked by

hand. They also used percussion caps and charges of gunpowder, which caused residue build-up and reduced their effectiveness. Several versions saw trial runs or actual battle service. The most widely used was the Williams machine gun, invented by a Confederate officer. According to Ian Drury,

> Self-consuming paper cartridges [each filled with gunpowder] were fed into the breech by hand and a percussion cap was placed on a nipple to the left of the chamber. The gun was operated by a crank and connecting rod that forced the breech block back and forth. By moving the crank the breech block

BODY ARMOR PROVOKES RIDICULE

In his entertaining book, Hardtack and Coffee, or, The Unwritten Story of Army Life, *published in 1887, John D. Billings, a Massachusetts artilleryman, recalled attempts by some soldiers to protect themselves with body armor.*

There were a good many men who were anxious to be heroes, but they were particular. They preferred to be *live* heroes. They were willing to go to war and fight as never man fought before, if they could only be insured against bodily harm. They were not willing to assume all the risks which an enlistment involved, without securing something in the shape of a drawback. Well, the iron tailors saw and appreciated the situation and sufferings of this class of men, and came to the rescue with a vest of steel armor,

worth, as I remember it, about a dozen dollars, and greaves [leg protectors]. The latter, I think, did not find so ready a market as the vests, which were comparatively common. These ironclad warriors admitted that when panoplied [armored] for the fight their sensations were much as they might be if they were dressed up in an old-fashioned air-tight stove; still, with all the discomforts of this casing, they felt a little safer with it on than off in battle, and they reasoned that it was the right and duty of every man to adopt all honorable measures to assure his safety in the line of duty. This seemed solid reasoning, surely; but in spite of it all, a large number of these vests never saw Rebeldom [i.e., battle with Rebel troops]. Their owners were subjected to such a storm of ridicule that they could not bear up under it.

The infamous Gatling gun had six separate barrels that rotated, firing in succession. The weapon foreshadowed the machine guns of the twentieth century.

was moved forward, chambering the cartridge and tripping the hammer. As the block came back, the hammer rose clear of the nipple once more and the process was repeated. [65]

Other experimental machine guns included the Agar gun, a single-barreled model that fed bullets into the breech via a circular ammunition hopper rotated by a hand crank, and the Gatling gun (invented by North Carolina's Richard J. Gatling), which featured six separate barrels that rotated and fired in succession.

These and other experimental weapons used in the war had little or no significant effect on its outcome. Yet in one way or another, they all ominously foreshadowed the more lethal face of future warfare. And some people argue that this fact alone is reason enough to view the Civil War as the first modern war.

Notes

Introduction: The First Modern War?

1. Joe H. Kirchberger, *The Civil War and Reconstruction: An Eyewitness History.* New York: Facts On File, 1991, p. viii.

2. Paddy Griffith, *Battle Tactics of the Civil War.* New Haven, CT: Yale University Press, 1989, pp. 15, 198.

3. A.A. Hoehling, *Damn the Torpedoes! Naval Incidents of the Civil War.* Winston-Salem, NC: John F. Blair, 1989, pp. 1, 9.

Chapter 1: Muskets and Rifles

4. Oscar L. Jackson, *The Colonel's Diary.* Privately printed, n.d., p. 73.

5. Archer Jones, *The Art of War in the Western World.* New York: Oxford University Press, 1987, pp. 269–70.

6. Ian Drury *The Civil War Military Machine: Weapons and Tactics of the Union and Confederate Armed Forces,* Illus. Tony Gibbons. New York: Smithmark, 1993, p. 50.

7. William B. Edwards, *Civil War Guns.* Harrisburg, PA: Stackpole, 1962, p. 15.

8. Drury, *The Civil War Military Machine,* p. 51.

9. Edward P. Alexander, *Military Memoirs of a Confederate.* New York: Scribner, 1907, pp. 52–53.

10. Alexander, *Military Memoirs,* p. 53.

11. Quoted in Time-Life, eds., *Arms and Equipment of the Union.* Alexandria, VA: Time-Life, 1991, p. 24.

12. Comte de Paris, *History of the Civil War in America.* Philadelphia: Porter and Coates, 1875, pp. 300–301.

Chapter 2: Artillery Guns and Batteries

13. Quoted in Time-Life, *Arms and Equipment of the Union,* p. 297.

14. Alexander, *Military Memoirs,* p. 53.

15. Drury, *The Civil War Military Machine,* p. 67.

16. Quoted in Warren Ripley, *Artillery and Ammunition of the Civil War.* New York: Van Nostrand, 1970, p. 118.

17. Quoted in Jack Coggins, *Arms and Equipment of the Civil War.* Garden City, NY: Doubleday, 1962, p. 64.

18. Coggins, *Arms and Equipment,* p. 63.

19. Quoted in Coggins, *Arms and Equipment,* p. 62.

20. Quoted in Kirchberger, *The Civil War and Reconstruction,* p. 106.

21. Quoted in Thomas B. Buell, *Combat Leadership in the Civil War.* New York: Crown, 1997, p. 89.

22. Quoted in Bruce Catton, *American Heritage New History of the Civil War.* New York: Viking, 1996, p. 54.

23. Quoted in Kirchberger, *The Civil War and Reconstruction,* p. 55.

24. Quoted in Kirchberger, *The Civil War and Reconstruction,* p. 55.

25. Coggins, *Arms and Equipment,* p. 96.

Chapter 3: Infantry Units and Tactics

26. Drury, *The Civil War Military Machine,* p. 22.

27. Drury, *The Civil War Military Machine,* p. 26.

28. Griffith, *Battle Tactics,* p. 149.

29. Griffith, *Battle Tactics,* p. 90.

30. Quoted in Otto Eisenschiml and Ralph Newman, *Eyewitness: The Civil War.* New York: Grosset and Dunlap, 1956, vol. 1, p. 441.

31. William C. Oates, *The War Between the Union and the Confederacy and Its Lost Opportunities.* New York: Neale, 1905, pp. 365–67.

32. Griffith, *Battle Tactics,* p. 138.

33. Griffith, *Battle Tactics,* pp. 132–33.

34. John W. de Forest, *A Volunteer's Adventures,* ed. J.H. Croushore. New York: Archon, 1970, p. 62.

35. Griffith, *Battle Tactics,* p. 143.

36. Charles E. Davis Jr., *Three Years in the Army.* Boston: Estes and Lauriat, 1894, p. 109.

Chapter 4: Cavalry Units and Tactics

37. Quoted in Drury, *The Civil War Military Machine,* p. 34.

38. Quoted in Coggins, *Arms and Equipment,* p. 48.

39. Quoted in Coggins, *Arms and Equipment,* p. 48.

40. Drury, *The Civil War Military Machine,* p. 36.

41. James McPherson, *Battle Cry of Freedom.* New York: Oxford University Press, 1988, p. 463.

42. Quoted in Henry S. Commager, ed., *The Blue and the Gray: The Story of the Civil War as Told by Its Participants.* New York: Bobbs-Merrill, 1950, p. 658.

43. Quoted in Commager, *The Blue and the Gray,* p. 661.

44. Quoted in Coggins, *Arms and Equipment,* p. 51.

45. Griffith, *Battle Tactics,* p. 180.

46. Quoted in Coggins, *Arms and Equipment,* p. 50.

Chapter 5: Ships and Naval Warfare

47. Coggins, *Arms and Equipment,* p. 126.

48. Commager, *The Blue and the Gray,* p. 796.

49. Quoted in Commager, *The Blue and the Gray,* p. 851.

50. Commager, *The Blue and the Gray,* p. 847.

51. Bern Anderson, *By Sea and River: The Naval History of the Civil War.* New York: Da Capo, 1989, pp. 71–72.

52. Quoted in Lydia M. Post, ed., *Soldiers' Letters from Camp, Battlefield, and Prison.* New York: Bunce and Huntington, 1865, p. 112.

53. Drury, *The Civil War Military Machine,* pp. 145–46.

54. Quoted in Commager, *The Blue and the Gray,* p. 818.

55. Anderson, *By Sea and River,* pp. 171–72.

Chapter 6: Espionage and Experimental Weapons

56. Edwin C. Fishel, *The Secret War for the Union: The Untold Story of Military Intelligence in the Civil War.* Boston: Houghton Mifflin, 1996, p. 8.

57. Donald E. Markle, *Spies and Spymasters of the Civil War.* New York: Hippocrene, 1994, p. 2.

58. Quoted in Alan Axelrod, *The War Between the Spies: A History of Espionage During the American Civil War.* New York: Atlantic Monthly Press, 1992, p. 45.

59. Quoted in Markle, *Spies and Spymasters,* p. 180.

60. Quoted in Markle, *Spies and Spymasters,* p. 179.

61. Axelrod, *The War Between the Spies,* p. 33.

62. Markle, *Spies and Spymasters,* p. 110.

63. Quoted in George A. Townsend, *Campaigns of a Non-Combatant, and His Romaunt Abroad During the War.* New York: Blelock, 1866, p. 117.

64. John D. Billings, *Hardtack and Coffee, or, The Unwritten Story of Army Life.* Boston: George M. Smith, 1887, p. 272.

65. Drury, *The Civil War Military Machine,* p. 64.

Glossary

aerial reconnaissance: Gathering information, usually of a military nature, from the air.

artillery: Cannons or ordnance.

battery: The main tactical unit of artillery; a Civil War artillery battery usually contained four to six cannons.

blockade runner: A ship that attempted to break through the Union's blockade of Southern ports.

bore: The inside of a gun's barrel.

breech: The back end of a gun's barrel.

breechloader: A firearm that loaded through the breech.

caliber: The specific width of a gun's bore.

canister: A cylindrical container filled with small musket balls or other metal objects that was fired by a cannon.

carbine: A shorter, lighter version of an ordinary rifle specially designed for use by cavalry.

company: An infantry unit comprising one-tenth of a regiment; a company contained about a hundred men.

espionage: Spying, or intelligence work.

fieldworks: Trenches defended and attacked by soldiers.

firefight: An exchange of fire by infantry units.

flank: The side or wing of a military formation.

flintlock: A mechanism for firing a gun in which a piece of flint strikes a piece of steel, producing a spark that ignites the gunpowder.

gun: In terms of artillery, a cannon with a long barrel that fired shot in low trajectories, best suited for use on an open battlefield where targets were in plain sight.

howitzer: A cannon with a barrel length falling between those of artillery guns and mortars; a howitzer could fire somewhat higher than an artillery gun.

intelligence: In military terms, information accumulated about one's enemy by spying or other means.

ironclad: A nineteenth-century warship whose hull was covered mainly by iron plates.

long arms: A general term for muskets, rifles, and carbines.

Maynard primer: A percussion-type firing system that used caps mounted on a tape that was cranked into place automatically.

Minié: A rifle bullet that expanded after the gun fired.

mortar: A cannon with a wide, short barrel designed for firing shells in a high trajectory, usually over fortress or city walls.

musket: An early gun with a smooth bore that fired by means of a flintlock or other mechanism.

muzzle: The front end of a gun's barrel.

Napoleon: A smoothbore artillery gun that was short and light, like a howitzer.

ordnance: Artillery or cannons.

percussion cap: A device for firing a gun; when the operator pulled the trigger, a metal hammer struck a metal plate coated with a chemical, which ignited, firing the weapon.

ram: A steam-powered vessel whose bow was reinforced so that it could ram enemy ships.

ramrod: A stick used to push the powder and ball down into the barrel of a musket or early rifle.

repeating rifle (or repeater): A rifle that used a cartridge containing multiple bullets that loaded automatically after each shot.

rifle: A gun with a rifled bore, or a barrel that has a set of spiral grooves etched on its inside.

rifle muskets: A general term for early military rifles.

saber: A slashing sword used mainly by cavalrymen.

shell: A metal container filled with gunpowder and fired from a cannon.

shock action: Direct assaults on enemy lines or defenses.

smoothbore: A firearm, such as the musket, that has a barrel with a smooth inside surface.

solid shot: A cannonball.

spar torpedo: A can of gunpowder attached to a pole extending from the bow of a submersible or semisubmersible.

spherical case: A round container filled with small musket balls or other metal objects and fired by a cannon.

submersible: A submarine; a semisubmersible was a warship with only a small portion of its hull showing above the waves.

torpedo: In the Civil War, a mine, either floating in the water or planted in a coal bin or some other place where it would explode and do damage.

trajectory: The flight path of a bullet or other missile.

troop: The basic unit of most U.S. cavalry in the nineteenth century; a troop varied in size from about seventy to a hundred men.

windage: In firearms, the space between the edge of the ball (or bullet) and the inside of the barrel.

For Further Reading

Jean F. Blashfield, *Horse Soldiers: Cavalry in the Civil War.* New York: Franklin Watts, 1998. An informative synopsis of cavalry in the war, aimed at junior high school readers.

Jim Murphy, *The Journal of James Edmond Pease: A Civil War Union Soldier, Virginia, 1863.* New York: Scholastic, 1998. The fascinating war recollections of a sixteen-year-old boy who joined the army.

Seymour Reit, *Behind Rebel Lines: The Incredible True Story of Emma Edmonds, Civil War Spy.* Fairbanks, AK: Gulliver Books, 2001. Tells how a twenty-one-year-old woman dressed as a man to enlist and proceeded to become a spy and master of disguise. Highly recommended.

John E. Stanchak, *Visual Dictionary of the Civil War.* London: Dorling Kindersley, 2000. Like so many other books by this publisher, this one is handsomely illustrated and provides a good starting point for young people learning about the subject for the first time.

Gail B. Stewart, *The Civil War: Weapons of War.* San Diego: Lucent Books, 2000. This commendable overview of the subject by a respected writer for young adults concentrates mainly on the political aspects of weapons development.

Time-Life, eds., *Civil War Battle Atlas.* Alexandria, VA: Time-Life, 1996. The editors of Time-Life have put together a colorful and useful book to guide general readers through a complex subject. The many maps and diagrams are first-rate, and each is accompanied by detailed explanations and background material.

G. Clifton Wisler, *When Johnny Went Marching Home: Young Americans Fight the Civil War.* New York: HarperCollins, 2001. Discusses the roles of cadets, drummers, and other young men in the conflict.

Major Works Consulted

Bern Anderson, *By Sea and River: The Naval History of the Civil War.* New York: Da Capo, 1989. A fine overview of the subject by a respected historian.

Alan Axelrod, *The War Between the Spies: A History of Espionage During the American Civil War.* New York: Atlantic Monthly Press, 1992. This absorbing volume is one of the better studies of intelligence gathering by both sides during the conflict.

Joseph G. Bilby, *Civil War Firearms.* Conshohocken, PA: Combined Publishing, 1996. A comprehensive synopsis of the wide and sometimes bewildering array of muskets, rifles, carbines, and pistols used in the war.

Jack Coggins, *Arms and Equipment of the Civil War.* Garden City, NY: Doubleday, 1962. This book by one of the great Civil War buffs was and perhaps remains the most widely read general summary of the weapons used in the conflict. Highly recommended.

Henry S. Commager, ed., *The Blue and the Gray: The Story of the Civil War as Told by Its Participants.* New York: Bobbs-Merrill, 1950. A massive volume containing hundreds of eyewitness accounts of Civil War events, battles, and people; an invaluable source for anyone engaging in a detailed study of the war.

Ian Drury, *The Civil War Military Machine: Weapons and Tactics of the Union and Confederate Armed Forces.* Illus. Tony Gibbons. New York: Smithmark, 1993. This excellent volume by historian Drury and illustrator Gibbons is somewhat more comprehensive than Coggin's older book (see above), especially in naval warfare.

William B. Edwards, *Civil War Guns.* Harrisburg, PA: Stackpole, 1962. An extremely detailed study of the firearms of the war; this book is sometimes laborious but is valuable for its comprehensiveness.

David J. Eicher, *The Longest Night: A Military History of the Civil War.* New York: Simon and Schuster, 2001. A large, detailed study of campaigns and battles of the war that tries to take into account much new information that has appeared since the publication of classics in the field, such as those by Bruce Catton, Shelby Foote (for both, see "Additional Works Consulted"), and James McPherson (see below). Eicher does not capture the epic sweep of the war the way the others do, but his book is worthwhile for its up-to-date information.

Edwin C. Fishel, *The Secret War for the Union: The Untold Story of Military Intelligence in the Civil War.* Boston: Houghton Mifflin, 1996. A huge, detailed look at the subject; this will appeal mainly to serious students and Civil War buffs.

Paddy Griffith, *Battle Tactics of the Civil War.* New Haven, CT: Yale University Press, 1989. Griffith, a noted English historian, delivers a first-rate study of the tactics used in the conflict; the work is especially strong in the way it relates military developments in America with those in Europe. Highly recommended.

Archer Jones, *Civil War Command and Strategy: The Process of Victory and Defeat.* New York: Free Press, 1992. This comprehensive discussion of the war's strategies and tactics is notable for its clear explanations of several difficult military concepts.

Philip Katcher, *American Civil War Artillery, 1861–1865.* 2 vols. Oxford: Osprey, 2001. Two detailed but very readable books covering a highly complex subject.

James McPherson, *Battle Cry of Freedom.* New York: Oxford University Press, 1988. This Pulitzer Prize–winning book is widely recognized as the best single-volume history of the Civil War. Highly recommended.

Grady McWhiney and Perry D. Jamieson, *Attack and Die: Civil War Military Tactics and the Southern Heritage.* Tuscaloosa: University of Alabama Press, 1982. Not as comprehensive and insightful as Griffith's book on tactics (see above), but still worthwhile.

Warren Ripley, *Artillery and Ammunition of the Civil War.* New York: Van Nostrand, 1970. A scholarly examination of the subject. General readers will prefer Philip Katcher's books (see above).

Additional Works Consulted

Edward P. Alexander, *Military Memoirs of a Confederate.* New York: Scribner, 1907.

Alfred Bellard, *Gone for a Soldier: The Civil War Memoirs of Private Alfred Bellard.* Ed. D.H. Donald. Boston: Little, Brown, 1975.

John D. Billings, *Hardtack and Coffee, or, The Unwritten Story of Army Life.* Boston: George M. Smith, 1887.

Henry N. Blake, *Three Years in the Army of the Potomac.* Boston: Lee and Shepard, 1865.

Ned Bradford, ed., *Battles and Leaders of the Civil War.* New York: Appleton-Century-Crofts, 1956.

Thomas B. Buell, *Combat Leadership in the Civil War.* New York: Crown, 1997.

Bruce Catton, *American Heritage New History of the Civil War.* New York: Viking, 1996.

———, *Glory Road.* New York: Doubleday, 1952. (The second volume of the monumental *Army of the Potomac* trilogy.)

———, *Mr. Lincoln's Army.* New York: Doubleday, 1952. (The first volume of the *Army of the Potomac* trilogy.)

———, *A Stillness at Appomattox.* New York: Doubleday, 1953. (The third volume of the *Army of the Potomac* trilogy.)

Charles E. Davis Jr., *Three Years in the Army.* Boston: Estes and Lauriat, 1894.

John W. de Forest, *A Volunteer's Adventures.* Ed. J.H. Croushore. New York: Archon, 1970.

Comte de Paris, *History of the Civil War in America.* Philadelphia: Porter and Coates, 1875.

Ian Drury, *Confederate Infantrymen, 1861–1865.* Oxford: Osprey, 1993.

Otto Eisenschiml and Ralph Newman, *Eyewitness: The Civil War.* 2 vols. New York: Grosset and Dunlap, 1956.

Shelby Foote, *The Civil War: A Narrative.* 3 vols. New York: Random House, 1958.

Arthur P. Ford, *Life in the Confederate Army.* New York: Neale, 1905.

Webb Garrison, *Strange Battles of the Civil War.* Nashville: Cumberland House, 2001.

———, *The Unknown Civil War.* Nashville: Cumberland House, 2000.

Rose Greenhow, *My Imprisonment and the First Year of Abolition Rule at Washington.* London: Richard Bentley, 1863.

Harry Hansen, *The Civil War: A History.* New York: New American Library, 1991.

Brian Hicks and Schuyler Kropf, *Raising the Hunley: The Remarkable History and Recovery of the Lost Confederate Submarine.* New York: Ballantine, 2002.

A.A. Hoehling, *Damn the Torpedoes! Naval Incidents of the Civil War.* Winston-Salem, NC: John F. Blair, 1989.

Oscar L. Jackson, *The Colonel's Diary.* Privately printed, n.d.

Archer Jones, *The Art of War in the Western World.* New York: Oxford University Press, 1987.

Philip Katcher, *Union Cavalrymen, 1861–1865.* Oxford: Osprey, 2000.

Oscar A. Kinchen, *Women Who Spied for the Blue and the Gray.* Philadelphia: Dorrance, 1972.

Joe H. Kirchberger, *The Civil War and Reconstruction: An Eyewitness History.* New York: Facts On File, 1991.

Donald E. Markle, *Spies and Spymasters of the Civil War.* New York: Hippocrene, 1994.

Peter S. Michie, ed., *The Life and Letters of Emory Upton.* New York: Appleton, 1885.

Samuel E. Morison, *The Oxford History of the American People.* New York: Oxford University Press, 1965.

William C. Oates, *The War Between the Union and the Confederacy and Its Lost Opportunities.* New York: Neale, 1905.

David D. Porter, *Naval History of the Civil War.* Secaucus, NJ: Castle, 1984.

Lydia M. Post, ed., *Soldiers' Letters from Camp, Battlefield, and Prison.* New York: Bunce and Huntington, 1865.

Time-Life, eds., *Arms and Equipment of the Confederacy.* Alexandria, VA: Time-Life, 1991.

———, *Arms and Equipment of the Union.* Alexandria, VA: Time-Life, 1991.

George A. Townsend, Campaigns of a Non-Combatant, and His Romaunt Abroad During the War. New York: Blelock, 1866.Cover: ©

Index

Picture Credits

Cover image: © Bettmann/CORBIS
The Art Archive, 27
© Bettmann/CORBIS, 20, 22, 83, 85,
© Richard A. Cooke/CORBIS, 48
© Tria Giovan/CORBIS, 25 (lower)
© Phillip Gould/CORBIS, 49
© CORBIS, 18, 45, 46, 50, 73,
© Getty Images, 17, 31, 58 (both), 61, 80,
Library of Congress, 11, 12, 21, 25 (upper), 34, 35, 36, 40, 53 (both), 62,
    63, 66, 68, 72, 74, 84, 86, 87 (both)
North Wind Picture Archives, 30, 32, 65, 69, 71, 75, 78, 89, 90
Steve Zmina, 14, 28, 37, 44, 70,
Stock Montage ,23, 39

About the Author

Historian and award-winning author Don Nardo has written many books for young adults about American wars, warfare, and weapons, including The *Mexican-American War, The War of 1812, The Indian Wars, World War II: The War in the Pacific,* and surveys of the weapons and tactics of the American Revolution. Mr. Nardo lives with his wife Christine in Massachusetts.